Franklin Reuben Elliott

Hand Book of practical Landscape gardening

Designed for city and suburban Residences, and country School-houses

Franklin Reuben Elliott

Hand Book of practical Landscape gardening
Designed for city and suburban Residences, and country School-houses

ISBN/EAN: 9783337242183

Printed in Europe, USA, Canada, Australia, Japan

Cover: Foto ©Andreas Hilbeck / pixelio.de

More available books at **www.hansebooks.com**

HAND BOOK

OF PRACTICAL

LANDSCAPE GARDENING

DESIGNED FOR

CITY AND SUBURBAN RESIDENCES,

AND COUNTRY SCHOOL-HOUSES,

CONTAINING

DESIGNS FOR LOTS AND GROUNDS,

From a lot 30 x 100 feet to a 40 acre plot.

Each plan is drawn to a scale, with schedule to each, showing where each Tree, Shrub, etc., should be planted. Also, Condensed Instructions of how to form Lawns, and the care thereof; the Building of Roads, Turfing, Protection of Trees, Pruning and care of, making Cuttings, Evergreens, Hedges, Screens, etc.; Perennials, Herbaceous Plants, etc. Also, Condensed Descriptions of all the leading Trees and Shrubs, with remarks as to soil and position in which they should be grown. Illustrations not only of the Ground Plans and Elevations are given, but Illustrations of various Trees, Shrubs, Winter Gardening, etc.

BY F. R. ELLIOTT,

LANDSCAPE GARDENER AND POMOLOGIST.

D. M. DEWEY,
HORTICULTURAL BOOKS, ARCADE HALL, ROCHESTER, N. Y.
1877.

Entered, according to Act of Congress, in the year 1877,
By D. M. DEWEY,
In the Office of the Librarian of Congress, at Washington.

C. H. STUMP & CO., PRINTERS,
Reynolds' Arcade, Rochester.

PREFACE.

In the preparation of this work we have aimed at no esthetical ideas; but believing that the people, as a whole, need some practical guide for the improvement and decoration of their home grounds, we have endeavored to make practical plans to a scale, and from which we think any man of ordinary intelligence can plant, according to the plan and schedule of varieties.

Since the labors of the lamented and talented A. J. DOWNING, great taste and desires for, and in the improvement of grounds around our homes, has been developed. The practical utility, as well as financial value of rural improvements is now fully understood; and all careful observers of the values of real estate concede that one per cent of value employed in decorating a rural home with appropriate walks and roads; with shade trees, shrubs and flowering plants judiciously arranged in the planting, will add forty per cent. to the value of the same when neglected. It is with this knowledge of the subject that we now present our work.

It is well known that a small cottage, with trees and flowering shrubs judiciously planted, is worth double the value of a two-story brick house, without any shade decorations around it. There are many who reside in these pleasant cottages around our country, that have more of real enjoyment than the man with a palace of $50,000 to $80,000.

There have been many elaborate works and well-designed plans, even going back one hundred years, but none of them have been adapted to the use of a plain, common-sense man, who can by measure, work to a scaled plan. The majority of the books on "*Landscape Gardening*" have, according to our knowledge, been made more for show, and as guides or exciting impulses to the man of wealth intellectually; but when the work has to be performed, a competent landscape gardener has to be employed.

In this work not only are our plans made to a scale, but each tree to be planted is designated by numbers. Again, in each plan we have given a ground plan design for a house and barn. The chapter on school-houses we hope will meet approval; and we thoughtfully hope and think that whoever looks over our work will give us credit, at least for trying to do good.

As a landscape gardener of forty years' practice, we feel like assuring those who follow our plans, that they will never regret the act.

F. R. E.

RURAL HOME ADORNMENTS.

The value of everything that approaches the beautiful, is enhanced by an appropriate setting. Even the most beautiful flower of nature is improved by its surrounding of delicately tinted green foliage. The artist, when exhibiting his most perfect artificial representation of nature, places it, if possible, with a surrounding which will measureably attract the eye, and yet cast upon the picture an enhanced breadth and height of coloring, combined with the softness which Nature in her hazy moods gives to all her productions.

Woman in all her beauty is rendered even more attractive in a setting of appropriate colors and forms of dress; and woe be to the taste of a blonde who, robing herself in light blue, seeks to decorate for relief with coral ornaments. The opaque red, to use a common phrase, would be "dreadful"; while the use of a pale pink would light up and dispel the pallid moonshine of the blue, and give to all a rich, pearly, hazy, rosy hue, as of early morn.

These lights and shades being well understood in our artificial "role," it would appear that in the more permanent matters of life, such as the decorations of our daily homes, they should have control; yet we too frequently find a mansion residence constructed after the best taste and truest principles of architecture, with its surrounding fitting as inappropriate as a bright yellow would be for a lady's walking dress.

OF THE FINE ARTS IN GENERAL AND LANDSCAPE GARDENING IN PARTICULAR.

There are many amateurs whose minds are open to conviction and inclined to truth, but whose powers of observation are not sufficient to enable them to discover what is right and appropriate, until it is pointed out to them.

The art of composition embraced in Landscape Gardening has certain principles which go towards forming a unity of the whole, and from which no deviation can be made without marring the result. Taste may be possessed in a greater or less degree; but without reference to principles it will fail to create a design of harmonious proportion or association. It is to be regretted that so little attention is given to the subject of principle and arrangement of tree, shrub, flower and path, as a whole in the decoration of our homes. Thousands on thousands of dollars are yearly expended in the creation of new places that have to be again remodeled because of apparent want, when completed, of congeniality and harmony necessary to an effective whole.

It is not expected that every man will or can be a landscapist, any more than he can be a lawyer or physician; but he should have sufficient love for his own home to induce him to study the principles of the art, so as to be able to appreciate the reasons for arrangements of designs submitted by a landscape artist. A spirit of independence, a pride and love for the creation of one's own, should imbue every citizen to the improvement by judicious planting of his home grounds. Were this the condition of things, the rapidity and beauty of new home surroundings would be greatly enhanced, and many grounds that now receive frequent remodeling would exhibit most gratifying results within a period of five to six years from first planting.

It may be pleasant to pass through an apprenticeship of learning by practice the character of tree and plant, the requisite breadth of lawn or road to give the best effect, or to arrange them in one harmonious whole, but it consumes years of time and is a knowledge which may be bought and made applicable whenever the purchaser has his ground ready for its practice. These prefatory remarks are as cautionary against one of the most common errors in ornamental gardening, viz: That of mixing herbaceous flowers with shrubs and trees, by which neither can thrive properly; or if they do, the effect of the one is injured by that of the other. However pleasing and picturesque it may be to see trees, shrubs and flowers all striving together for the mastery in a natural wood, yet this sort of beauty is totally unsuited to scenes of art; and however much the owner may desire to see and study every tree, shrub and flower, it is better to plant the surplus in a reserve border in some part of the rear garden, than to destroy unity and effect by a crowding of varieties incongruously together. Another error common to small gardens is the want of some leading feature of special interest, such as the creating of a flower-garden proper, a fountain, or rockery; the two last named are the most difficult, and require a tasteful, experienced landscape artist to execute them so that they remain permanent and beautiful ornaments, harmonizing with the surrounding grounds.

The flower garden proper, as well as the floral beds, are readily constructed and within the power of all. More or less of these should be placed near the house so that more or less of views from the windows of the house will look down upon them. Various patterns for the arrangement of the beds and paths are found in all works on landscape gardening, but in copying them thought should be taken as to their adaptation to the position or form of boundary in which they are to be placed. In most of the plans in this work we have given specific designation of what and where to plant. We will now turn to a few short hints as to how to do the work in the forming of a new place:

The Verge of Walks and Roads should always be made as inconspicuous as possible. The less the verge is elevated above the walk, the less we have of harsh line to break the smoothness and harmony of blending from lawn to roadway or flower-bed. Some gardeners seem to think that a strong, harsh line, or verge of two inches deep or more, next the path, is a mark of skill; but to our taste it is only an exhibit of mechanical labor breaking in upon the softness of Nature's own laws, which always resolve into one another without any harsh or offending feature. The verge to a path should rise from the path just as little as possible, if even extra care have been taken to cut each line sloping underneath, as it were, so that when the roller is passed over it, the line of demarkation will be perceptible only by the change of gravel to turf.

Roll the Walks and Roads.—Frequent rolling of the pathways during winter is essential to keeping them firm and smooth. It matters not whether they are traveled upon or not, they should be rolled over every time when the frost is out of the surface two inches or more. The same should be done after every rain during the open seasons of the year.

Garden Soil will always pay for trenching deep, even if done with the spade; but remember to keep all the time the good or surface soil at the top, and not bury it at the bottom, as we have seen done by some gardeners. If the expense of trenching the whole garden this year be too much for the purse, then select one portion for this season's improvement and another for next year. Clay soils are especially benefited by trenching, and while such soils are not specially adapted to early crops, the trenching will be found a great aid in the aeration it gives toward earliness, and for a dry, hot summer a clay soil trenched is superior to any of lighter texture.

Deciduous Trees and Shrubs should be planted just as early in the season as the ground will work freely. Do not delay; for although many a tree succeeds when transplanted late in the season, should an unfavorable season occur, it will not grow as vigorously, and frequently gets so small a hold in the soil, that although alive at the commencement of winter, spring finds it without vitality sufficient to make a new growth.

Turfing New Grounds.—When turf is to be laid, the ground should be permitted to lay and settle during one or two good rains before the turf is put on, otherwise it will settle unevenly and the turf be full of holes. After the ground has become well settled, rake it over anew and level again; then roll, and again rake as you lay the turf. Laying the turf irregularly, or rather with intervening spaces of one to two inches wide, and filling with soil, then seeding with grass seed and rolling all down together, is now practiced pretty generally and with great success in its results. No beating is given to the sod—the roller doing all the pressure needed to form a good surface.

Seed for Lawns.—Let the ground be first thoroughly prepared, that is, dug at least one foot—better to be eighteen inches—deep, and all of this depth to be of good, rich, loamy soil, not ten inches of poor clay or sand with two inches of top dressing, but all the depth of good loam suitable for growing a heavy crop of corn or a bed of carrots; make the whole depth and quality of soil uniform, without regard to the rise and fall of the grades; in other words, do not form the soil in one place fourteen inches deep and in another only ten, and then calling it an average of one foot; because the lawn hereafter will tell of your work by its exhibit of rich green grass in the deep soil places and of yellow dried spots in the shallow ones; but make it all an even, regular depth, whether on a rising knoll or a low level grade. Rake and pulverize with the roller all the top surface as fine as an ash heap. When ready for sowing, procure for one acre—or in proportions according to the surface to be seeded—two bushels of Blue Grass, two bushels of Red Top, half a bushel of Creeping Bent, and one-eighth bushel of White Clover; mingle them well together, and then divide into three equal parts. Sow first one part; then go over the ground with a fine rake, say from north to south, raking the whole surface back and forth to lightly cover the seed; then sow another third portion of the seed and repeat the raking cross-wise, or from east to west; then sow the last remaining portion of seed, and with a heavy roller, roll or press the whole surface, both for the purpose of cementing the seed in the soil for vegetating, and also to prevent measurably the wash liable to accrue from rains. We sometimes see advice of one bushel of seed to an acre; again, of two or three, with a sprinkling of rye, as they say, to shade the young grass—the adviser probably forgetting that the strong, rank roots of the rye do more injury by extraction of moisture and food from the roots than the benefit, if there is any, obtained from its shade. London, we believe, was in the practice of using from six to eight bushels of seed to the acre; Downing, from four to six; and our experience of twenty years over many and many an acre is, that if a good firm lawn is expected the first year, it is always unsafe to use less than four bushels, and that the addition of one or two bushels more well pays in the thick nest of grass readily grown and the lessening of labor in extracting weeds that, where no grass is, will surely grow. A top dressing of bone meal, ten bushels to the acre, with two bushels of salt and one-half bushel of gypsum (plaster), will also always be found a profitable expenditure.

Grass Lawns.—When newly made must not be so closely mown as old turf, but mowing must be performed with regularity, or it is impossible to obtain a uniform velvety green surface. To mow close a well-established turf is to encourage the fine grasses and kill out the coarse kinds. Salt and plaster are good manures. Use at the rate of one bushel of plaster and three bushels of salt to the acre, and sow just before a rain. To have a good lawn, it should be freely mown, and no matter how closely, early in the season; but as soon as the hot season comes on, the mowing should be less frequent and less close; while during August, care should be had to rolling it often and early in the morning, while the dew is on and the mowing high, or just so that no seed be formed. As soon as the fall rains commence, then the lawn may be closely mown again; but near the close of the season it should be left to form a growth for a winter coat of protection to the crowns of the roots. These remarks will be found in practice just as applicable where command of water for sprinkling is had as where it is not. The result, however, will not as soon develop.

Keep the Surface of the Ground Loose.—We have many years watched the varied results of the cultivator who keeps frequently stirring the surface of his soil, and the one who hoes or cultivates only when the weeds compel him to the work; and as we have watched and recorded our notes, the result has always been in favor of the constant stirring of the surface soil. We do not advocate deep tillage during the growing season, but we would have the ground deeply and thoroughly stirred early in the season, whether it were an old or new plantation. Once, however, that vigorous growth of top and root has commenced, all deep tillage should cease, because, by pursuing it, constant and continued checks are given, and a truly healthy growth prevented by repeated breaking and tearing asunder the roots and fibers, the supplying pipes for elongation, expansion and evaporation of the branches and leaves. By repeated surface stirring of the soil, however, no roots are broken; the sun, air and moisture are enabled to penetrate and assist in the chemical transmutation of the earth's compounds, and fitting them for absorption by the roots.

Protect the Crowns of Trees.—Experience is a good teacher, and it has taught us that the action of severe frosts, followed by rapid thaws on the surface roots and crowns of trees, creates very great injury, often resulting in death. We have known trees healthy on approach of winter, and the same when dug in spring; we have found them with all the top and the lower roots uninjured, but the crown and surface roots entirely blackened and dead. This is often a result with grape-vines—in fact, we have seen hundreds of vines exhibit this condition. During the past autumn we have repeatedly urged the earthing up to the crowns of trees and plants, with a view to prevention of this result. We now say, look over your trees carefully, and if you have not turned the earth toward them, thus covering the surface roots and crowns two or three inches deeper than their position during the growing season, you should now do it by a mulch of some sort. In the forest, Nature herself performs this act by the dropping of the leaves; but in the open ground, unless the trees stand in turf, and the fall growth of grass is left, no such protection is had. Surface-rooting plants, such as the quince, Paradise apple, etc., and all newly-planted vines or plants, suffer greater injury, because of the greater number of surface roots than older or stronger rooted plants; but all are affected, and the severity of the winter and number of changes of frost and thaws will tell the result the next season—sometimes in enfeebled growth, sometimes in complete death.

Pruning Trees in Spring.—When pruning trees in the spring, remember that for every bud or inch of wood you cut away, two more will be formed; and if you do not so cut as to throw the elongation from the last bud on the shoot left in an outward direction, your tree will soon be a mass of shoots and branches, and cause you to oppose any practice of pruning. On the other hand, if you carefully study the probable continuation of each bud left at the end of the shoot pruned, you can form your tree into a round, open, compact or spreading head, according to your fancy. We could write a whole book on this item; but our belief is that a few practical words of guidance are all that is requisite to induce thought in the good common sense of our readers.

Winter Pruning.—We do not advocate winter pruning, because we think the wound made by the cut at this time more liable to dry, and crack, and open, exposing it to water lodgment as well as to harden at the edge, more than when performed early in autumn or just as the sap starts in spring. If, however, winter pruning has to be done, the operator should select a time when the temperature, if possible, is above freezing point, and in the middle of the day, and even then we would never cut away any large or strong limbs at this time.

Plow up to the Roots of Trees and Vines.—All young orchard trees, grape-vines, raspberries, blackberries, gooseberries, etc., should have the earth either plowed or shoveled up toward them, leaving the center line between rows as a surface water-line for winter drainage. Breaking of the roots by the plow in autumn will not injure the plants, trees or vines, so that the laborer need not be afraid of going too deep with plow or spade. Leave the ground as rough as it will naturally lie,—in other words, do not rake and smooth down after plow or spade, because, when left rough, the action of the elements during winter serves almost as good a purpose as a light dressing of manure.

Bush and Pyramid Trees, under the common name of dwarfs, should be carefully watched and pinched back from time to time, if any special form is desired to be retained.

Shrubs under Drip of Trees.—It sometimes becomes necessary to plant some shrubs under the shade and drip of trees, in order to make up for the loss of branches, etc. The Daphne mezereum, Mahonia aquifolia, Hypericum percinum, barberries of all sorts, and also privet, are good plants for the purpose. For covering the ground in the summer, in places where the grass fails to succeed, the varieties of vinca, of ribbon grass, Hypericum hirsutum and Irish ivy are among the many good vines and creepers that may be used.

Hardy Shrubs are readily propagated from cuttings of the present year's growth of wood.

It is better to make cuttings of all hardy shrubs, as currants, gooseberries, wieglas, spiræas, etc., in the autumn than to delay until mid-winter or spring. At this time the wood and bud are all in full health and capable of sustaining themselves into growth in spring independent of the root; but late in winter they are often so much enfeebled by exhaustion and exposure to extremes of cold, that often they fail to grow even under the best of care. This loss of vitality, if the shoot or bud were left on the parent plant, would be renewed in the spring by means of the roots, but when separated therefrom, can not be replaced, and hence the cause for a too oft failure in growing winter-made cuttings. Cuttings early in Autumn may be at once planted out in the open ground where they are to grow, and covered entirely first with earth, then over it with a light character of mulch, as straw, meadow hay, etc., the mulch to be removed in spring and the earth also down to a strong bud. Or the cuttings may be tied in bundles and packed in clean sand in a cool cellar or pit, or they may be packed away in thin layers, with moss intervening, and so kept for planting out in early spring.

Roses Propagated by means of Layers should, as soon as it is certain they have become rooted, be taken up and potted off in good sharp, rich, sandy soil. It is no trick to form the layer, but many rose-growers know to their cost the loss attendant during winter of layered plants taken up and potted or heeled in at the close of the growing season. Pot them as soon as they have made an inch of root; set them in a shady place, water carefully for a few days, or until there is no appearance of their flagging, when the pots may be plunged in the soil, out in the full light, and by the close of the season each will present a well-grown and bushy plant. Of course they must be occasionally watered.

Evergreens, where they can be procured from a near-by nursery, may be removed with almost sure success during October. The trees have completed their growth, and the soil being warm when removed, the broken roots will heal and form new roots much more rapidly than in spring, when the earth is cold. Keep the roots from even a half hour's drying; and when planting, thoroughly saturate the ground immediately in connection with copious watering, before completely filling in all the earth. If a rainy time occur, the artificial watering may be dispensed with. If but a few trees are to be removed, the operator can almost always select a cloudy or drizzling, rainy day, when, if it is not quite so pleasant working, there is less care required to keep the roots from drying, and the application of water by hand can be entirely dispensed with.

Perennials.—October month is one of the best for transplanting and dividing perennial plants; and as flowering perennials are among the easiest cultivated in forming a flower garden, and abound in great diversity of foliage and color of flower, they should be freely planted in every garden. Prepare the ground by digging it fully one foot deep, and mingling—unless already rich—a quantity of well decomposed manure or compost. Obtain the plants from a reliable dealer—order good strong roots—plant them carefully, and then spread a light covering of coarse straw manure, say two inches deep, over all for winter protection.

Hollyhocks.—The production of seedling varieties of the hollyhock has been very great during the past ten years, and at this time they equal, if they do not surpass, in beauty the dahlia. They are perfectly hardy, and can be left in the open border with impunity. Seeds of choice kinds sown early in the season in a hot-bed frame, and got ready for transplanting in May, will flower the same season; while divisions and cuttings from choice varieties already produced may be made, and by giving them a slight start in a frame, will transplant and bloom finely, forming one of the cheapest and most effective background features for a flower garden imaginable. Make the ground deep and rich with abundance of well rotted cow-dung.

Herbaceous Plants.—Hardy herbaceous plants should be transplanted as early as the ground can be worked freely. After planting, cover the crowns with an inch or two of leaf mold or chip dirt, as it will greatly assist them in resisting the freezing and thawing until the full opening of spring. In digging over beds of herbaceous plants, be careful, as many plants like peonias, campanulas, etc., are often destroyed by spading or forking, and thus destroying their crowns ere they have shown their buds above ground. It is always well to be in time; but better wait a day or two more rather than dig, until each plant can be distinctly traced in its position.

Herbaceous Plants, as soon as they have done flowering, may be easily propagated by cuttings. These should be planted in a cold frame in a mixture of sand and loam, and kept shaded until roots have formed.

Hardy Annuals.—In selecting varieties of hardy annuals, seek rather a few of those that bloom freely and grow vigorously, than to make your collection one of varieties. Very little satisfactory effect can be obtained from a great variety, many of them possessing no distinctive character of color, however pretty and curious they may be to the botanist. Large masses of a few sorts and of distinct colors, white, crimson etc., such as candytufts, phlox-Drummondi, etc., will give, are very effective either in small gardens or on extensive lawns.

Bedding Plants require special attention to pinching and pegging, for on this depends greatly the beauty of display as the plants come into bloom.

A Bed of Lilies.—By all means plant out a bed of Japan lilies. Select, if you can, a position where when they come into flower you will have to look up rather than down to see the flower; make the ground two feet or more deep, working into it plenty of well-rotted compost manure; then get the varieties of lily in all their numbers; plant them at distances of about one foot apart each way, setting the bulb in clean sand and covering about three inches deep.

We have been at one time particularly observant of two beds of Japan lilies in a neighbor's garden,—one growing in the ordinary open exposed garden bed, the other planted among some rock work on the north side of the house. The first blooms a few days the earliest, but the flowers are soon gone, while the latter continues in bloom nearly six weeks.

This is a significant hint to planters of hardy bulbs, as it means that the latter bed has moisture and depth for the roots, sustaining their growth for a long period, while the former, by reason of open exposure, are enhanced perhaps in period of blooms, but from the heat are brought rapidly to maturity. Planters of lilies, therefore, should, in order to have abundant and long continued blooms, dig the ground very deep, and in spring, or just before blooming time, shield the surface by a light surface mulching.

Soil for Lilies.—In the ordinary prepared soils of eight inches deep, for the Japan lilies, the growth of flower stems varies from eighteen inches to two feet in height; but where the ground is prepared some eighteen inches deep, of rich soil and drained, the flower stems rise to four and five feet, and with proportionate increase of flowers. Lilium auratum has been grown with stems nine feet high, and having nineteen perfect flowers upon it, some of which have measured one foot in diameter.

Hoe with the Rake.—This may be an Irishman's advice, but we have found great advantage in the use of an iron tooth rake or toothed hoe during the early cultivation of all garden crops. We go over our beets, parsnips, peas, beans, etc., with a twelve tooth steel rake as soon as they show sign of coming above ground. For potatoes, corn, and for working among raspberries and other small fruits, and for stirring the surface earth around dwarf pears and recently planted trees, we use a four-pronged hook or hoe, with which a man will perform nearly or quite one sixth more work in a day, destroy the weeds, and leave the ground always light, loose and even.

CONDENSED DESCRIPTIONS OF TREES AND SHRUBS.

We commence this list with the Evergreen trees and shrubs or creepers. The trees are valuable as screens from cold winds, hedges, and as features of beauty and of back-grounds in the creation of beautiful home grounds, and especially do they give life ideal in the winter. A tall symmetrical evergreen in winter, laden with frozen snow, in the early rays of the morning sun or the soft, silvery light of the moon, can never be seen without feeling that all of beauty comes from the good God's creation, not man's artifice. Many places, however, are rendered gloomy and dark from their too free use in the foreground and near to the house. Many have planted beautiful Norway spruces of three feet high within eight feet of their front windows, or three feet of their walks or roadways, forgetting that in half a dozen to a dozen of years they will be from twenty to thirty feet high, and as many of breadth of limb base. The same silly thing has been done on lots in a cemetery of 12 by 20 feet.

In evergreens there is a great deal of beauty, especially in winter, but as a class for effective scenery, creative of varied beauty in months when deciduous trees are in bud, bloom and foliage. They have not the qualities of a change in character from month to month of the deciduous trees and shrubs. They can be grouped beautifully with the Mountain Ash, Euonymus or Strawberry tree, which bear clusters of red fruit in late autumn and winter.

In removing and transplanting evergreens the first statement was, that they should have balls of earth attached, the next was that they could only be moved at certain seasons of the year; but those who practically and theoretically understand the evergreen tree or plant, can move them at any time when the ground can be worked freely, except the months of July and August, in all our latitudes from above 43° down to 40°, below that June and September must be included with July and August. In transplanting, it is only requisite to remember that the tree has its leaves on, and that there is consequently a constant demand upon the roots for evaporation by the leaves, and therefore it will not do to permit them to get *dry.* With small sized trees, a root nearly corresponding with the top is generally procured, when the trees have been rightly grown in the nursery and cutting in of the top is unnecessary; but in the case of removal of trees six feet or more in height, unless extraordinary care is taken, a great reduction of the root is the result, and then it is advisable always to shorten in the length of the branches corresponding with the apparent loss of roots the tree has sustained.

The writer of this has superintended the removal of evergreen trees thirty feet in height, and breadth according at the base. The practice has been to first mark the outline of the lower branches, then raise them gently and carefully and tie them points upward at six feet above the ground by a soft rope or strap passed once around and fastened to the main stem of the tree; then with rakes and forks take off the surface ground among the small fibrous roots to a depth of four inches, then dig a trench eighteen inches deep and wide at the outskirt line of the branches; this done, then work underneath the roots and carefully loosen them until they can be raised and tied to the body of the tree—then place a mat underneath, and if the tree has to go any distance pack wet moss among the roots, if it is only to be moved one-quarter of a mile, merely sprinkling the roots and wetting the mat will be necessary. Have the hole for its transplanting ready dug and well wet, then set the tree upon a little mound for its center and take down the roots one by one and spread them as near to their natural position as can be done, mingling soil by pressure of the fingers outspread, not jammed down with the fist or a club stick. Avoid all treading of the feet, but with the hand outspread see to it that the base has no vacancy from packed soil of even one inch diameter.

Follow this with each course of roots, having calculated that your upper tier will be four inches below the level of the ground and your tree with one careful watering like rain—not inch jets—and a mulch of four inches of new mown grass, straw, sawdust or tanbark, is all right. Not a stake is needed. Having said so much touching the evergreens, we shall now take up our

CONDENSED DESCRIPTIONS.

American Arbor Vitæ.—This is commonly known as White Cedar, but it does not belong botanically to that class. It is a hardy evergreen, conical, upright, uniform; excellent for screens and hedges and can, by clipping annually, be grown in any form. Small plants of it, by judicious yearly pruning, can be kept at a height of three to four feet, with a spread of thirty feet diameter.

American Weeping Arbor Vitæ.—This is of small, say half natural habit in size, of a drooping habit; rare and beautiful.

Arbor Vitæ—Var Ericoides.—Is a dwarf variety, with heath-like foliage; suited only to rock work, or some groups of dwarf evergreens.

Arbor Vitæ—Hoveyi.—This is a variety of our common American; more compact and dwarf in its habit.

Arbor Vitæ—Maculata.—A blotched leaved variety of the American; only of value as a curiosity.

Arbor Vitæ—Plicata.—A variety with a dark green foliage; untested.

Arbor Vitæ—Plicata Minima.—Said to be a dwarf of the foregoing.

Arbor Vitæ—Siberica.—This is one of the hardiest, most perfect in growth and habit of the whole class of *Thujas*. It matters not where it is placed, or what you want of it; a knowledgeable person can use it in any form or position. There is a variety with variegated foliage, suited to a novelty tree or plant grower.

Arbor Vitæ—Tom Thumb.—Botanically this has no distinct designation, but the plant is distinct, and for a compact symmetrical grower it has no equal. It deserves a place in every man's grounds, and thousands of them should be used in cemeteries. It originated in Ellwanger & Barry's gardens, Rochester, N. Y.

Arbor Vitæ—Chinese.—Some place this as botanically *Biota*, instead of *Thuja*. In many sections it is one of our most delicate shrub evergreen trees, and may be trained to any form. It often browns in winter, but with careful clipping in early spring it comes out beautiful with its clear light green. We have grown it conical, oval, flat and rounded.

Arbor Vitæ—Compacta.—This is a variety of the Chinese, but more dwarf and compact in its natural form. It is hardy.

Arbor Vitæ—Golden.—A variety of the Chinese, with foliage of a yellowish hue; beautiful, and said to be hardy—of which we have doubts.

Arbor Vitæ—Pygmea.—A very dwarf variety. There are many more of these, but when we work for the benefit of the public we do not feel like wasting time noting novelties untested.

Cypress—Cupressus Lawsoniana.—This is one of the most graceful of evergreen trees. It is not, however, fully hardy in all locations, but deserves a place where some other evergreens shade and protect it from the sun in winter. Like the Chinese Arbor Vitæ it requires to have the ends of some of the twigs clipped in spring.

There are several other varieties more erect and compact. One *Stricta* is among the best. *McNabiana* has glaucous leaves. *Nutkaensis* has glossy, dark green foliage, and is very beautiful. *Thyoides* is the true white cedar, quite hardy. There are two or more of Japan Cypress, but their hardihood is not yet fully tested.

Juniper—(Juniperus.)—All of this class are hardy and valuable. They are of all forms, from lowest creeper to tall stately trees, like the Red cedar.

Juniperus Virginiana.—These are very erect dwarf varieties, and drooping, almost weeping.

Libocedrus.—Of this class there are but two varieties, viz.: *Chiiensis* and *Decurrens*, both handsome, but not hardy at the North.

Pines.—Nearly all of the pines are hardy. The Mountain, (*Mugho*,) *Mugho Rotundata* and Dwarf White Pine (*Strobus Nana*) are among the hardest and best of dwarfs. The Austrian, White, Norway or Red, Scotch, Corrican, Banksian and Swiss Stone are perfectly hardy. The five first named make large beautiful trees, each distinct in color of foliage, the two last named (Banksian) is of a yellowish cast in foliage, a half drooping in form, Swiss Stone or Cembrian is of a light whitish green, like unto the White or Monmouth pine, yet more compact and upright. Both this and Banksia make only small trees.

The Bhotan (Excelsa) is a variety of great beauty, but it must be planted in dry and poor ground and shaded or sheltered from the sun in winter by evergreen or buildings. Salzmann's, Bentham's, Heavy-wooded, Jeffrey's and Lambert's are all of recent introduction, and give promise of forming some of the most stately and hardy trees. The Calabrian is one of the most beautiful of all, but it is very rare. The Russian (*Rigensis*) is much like Bentham, yet distinct, is hardy and vigorous, more open than the Austrian; foliage yellowish green, bright and clear.

Silver Fir—Picea.—The American Balsam Fir is well-known, and while young makes fine trees, as it acquires age, however, it should have the ends of its branches clipped yearly. The variety called Hudson Bay Fir makes only a dwarf tree. The European or *Pectinata* and also *Webbiana* are liable to lose their leading stems, especially while young. The *Amabilis*, Cephalonican, Cilician, Great Silver, Noble, Nordmann's, Pinsapo and Wooly-fruited are among the more recent introductions and worthy of attention.

Spruce Fir.—The American White Spruce is one of the most beautiful of hardy trees, second class in size. The American is

of a darker shade in foliage, and more upright in its branches.
Both are valuable as screen hedges, or dwarf evergreen hedges,
as they bear the shears well. *Alba Cerulea, Excelsa Clan-
brasiliana, Elegans, Gergoryana, Mucronata, Parviformis, Pygmœa,
Canadenis Nana, Pumila, Nigra, Tortuosa Compacta* are all classed
as dwarf trees.

The Excelsa Inverta is a pendulous variety of the Norway
Spruce. The commonly well-known Norway Spruce and the
Hemlock Spruce are too well known to need a word. Both are
of value as specimen trees, wind breaks or hedges. There are a
number of other varieties, but none superior to those we have
named, unless it be the Himalayan.

Sequoia Gigantea.—This is called the big tree of California, is
majestic in form, but too often it proves unreliable north of 42
latitude, below that it is all right, and situations, soils, with care
can grow it at the North.

The Yew—Taxus.—This evergreen is all of the dwarf form.
There are rare foliaged varieties and many very compact, but
nearly all of them brown badly from winter suns. The English
(*Baccata*) and Irish (*Hibernica*) sometimes grow to a height of 20
to 30 feet. The *Nana, Stricta, Adpressa* are among the best as
low shrubs, and *Dovastonii pendula* is fine as a weeping variety.

WEEPING DECIDUOUS TREES.

Within a few years the popular taste has been largely turned
to the introduction of drooping trees as objects of graceful
beauty, harmonizing with the smoothness and verdue of a lawn,
or the high keeping and neatness of a pleasure garden. Drooping trees, like water fountains, are dangerous in the hands of
those who attempt their use in the decoration of grounds, without possessing a considerable knowledge and good taste in the
composition of a landscape. Gracefulness and elegance being
the prominent characteristics of drooping trees, they are shown
to the best advantage either singly or in wide, yet tasteful
groups, or lawns, or borders; where symmetrical art, rather than
the natural picturesque is sought to be embodied as the leading

feature, where bold expression is desired, they are entirely unfitted. Placed on the borders of groups, at sufficient distance to enable them to exhibit their peculiar habits and develop freely their forms, many of the drooping trees may be used effectively, provided the group of which they form a part is composed with similar pensile, although not so distinct in habits of foliage or spray as exhibited in the American elm, black birch, or wild cherry. For planting on the borders of ponds, or streams of running water, or as symbols of sympathy between the living and the dead in cemeteries, they are all valuable; and with judicious knowledge of their expansion in growth to arrange them on lots or in positions suitable to their future lives, they cannot be too much used.

VARIETIES.

European Weeping Ash.—This is one of the oldest varieties of weeping trees known. Originally it was more extensively planted than any other variety, because of its rapid growth and clear, glossy foliage. There are also of Weepers the gold barked and the Lentiscus-leaved, both valuable, but in sections not quite hardy.

Weeping Beech.—This we consider the king of all the weeping trees. It is perfectly hardy, grows freely and rapidly in almost any soil, and forms one of the most graceful and picturesque, yet unique trees.

European Weeping Birch.—The cut-leaved Weeping Birch is one of the best of this variety. Among the new varieties the *Elegans pendula* and Young's New Weeping are entirely distinct, yet of the most delicate character.

Weeping Cherry.—Of this class we give preference to the dwarf weeping *(pumila)* and the ever flowering *(semperflowrens)*. Both require to be grafted from four to six feet high.

Weeping Cypress—Cupressus Glyptostrobus pendula.—This is a beautiful weeper, but we regard it as not hardy at the North.

Weeping Elm.—Of the Weeping Elms we count the Camperdown as the most persistent drooping drooping variety. The

Scotch Weeping has drooping branches but not pendulous. The cork barked is distinct, so also Hertfordshire and rough leaved. The small leaved is only of value for the reserve garden as a study.

Weeping Euonymous.—This is a variety of a shrub called the Strawberry tree or Burning Bush. It is a novelty of value.

Weeping Honey Locust.—Hardy and with fine foliage, but we should award it a place only in the reserve grounds.

Weeping Larch.—If a tree is wanted for a rocky bank, or as a grotesque feature at some conspicuous point nothing can equal the Weeping Larch, but for a symmetrical lawn it is not suited.

Weeping Linden.—The tree that goes under the name of Weeping Linden is not strictly a weeper. Its foliage is whitish underneath and with age it has a half drooping habit.

Weeping Mountain Ash.—This is one of the most beautiful of weeping trees, but the *Saperda*, a borer, often destroys it by girdling it. It is generally worked upon the common Mountain ash at six to eight feet high, and in four years its branches reach the ground, loaded with white blooms in spring and red berries in winter.

Weeping Poplar.—The variety of this weeper (*grandidenta pendula*) is well adapted to the back-ground of a group of weepers, but it is too strong and bold, except upon a large lawn or back from a pond or running stream.

Weeping Sophora.—The *Sophora Japonica Pendula* is one of the most beautiful of weepers. The foliage is smooth, dark green, with very pendulous branches and pinnate leaves. Occasionally trees of it stand hardy in our Northern latitude, but above 42° we should never advise its planting.

Weeping Willows.—The *Salix Babylonica* is our old well-known weeping willow. From long usage this willow has come to be associated with either water or the sadness of life—in the one case, indicative of a marshy region or stream of water; in the other, of the last resting place of friends once on earth. Beautiful as it is in itself, these very associations preclude its introduction into almost any suburban or even extended place.

The American or Fountain Willow and the Kilmarnock come in well at times on the point where two roads meet and converge. They are also adapted to borders and corners of lots in cemeteries. Two owners of lots adjoining should conspire together to place the weeper upon the joint corner line.

Weeping Thorn.—There are several varieties of Weeping Thorns (*Crategus*) all of them pretty and well suited for planting on small lawns or cemetery lots.

DECIDUOUS TREES.

In all of ornamental gardening the deciduous trees take a first rank for the blossoming of the bud, the ripening of the seed or fruit, the ever changing of the foliage gives daily a variety to the whole of the grounds where they are planted. Our work is not of sufficient extent of character to note all varieties, unless we condense our remarks to a few words.

The Snowy Maple Leaved Abele, belonging to the poplar family, is a tree of rapid growth, but with such a tendency to sucker that it is unworthy of culture.

The Ailanthus, or Flower of Heaven, is a tree of rapid growth. Like others, elm, maple, etc., it has two sexes, both of which produce flowers, the male much less abundantly than the female, and while the male suckers freely the female does not. The perfume from the flower of the female is poisonous, while that of the male is not. No insects trouble these trees, and they are mainly valuable for the street.

The Ash is varied in its forms and accordingly is suited to locations. The flowering *Var, Ornus Europea, Salicifolia, Americanus* are among the best for lawns or streets. An ornamental tree is produced by grafting the Dwarf Globe *headed* (originated with Ellwanger & Barry) about six feet high on the stocks of the American Ash.

The Beech—Fagus.—Our American Beech (*Fagus Americana*) we rank as combining in itself more of beauty, grace and magnificence than perhaps any other of our forest trees. True, it has not the oak, but with its stateliness of upright, spreading growth, every line and twig is one of graceful ease. Young trees should always be procured with branches starting from the ground, and rarely does it need the knife applied to give it regularity and symmetry and form. A deep, loamy, rather moist soil gives it most vigor and causes it to grow to a large size. As a single lawn tree it has no superior, and wherever room can be given for its full development it should be planted.

There are mady varieties of the Beech, of which the Cut leaved, Crested leaved, Fern leaved, Long leaved, Oak leaved and Purple leaved, each have a distinct character. The Purple leaved is certainly the most desirable of all, except the native. It has rather stronger limbs than the common plain variety, and the young shoots and buds are of a rare color, while the foliage, when young or half grown, is of a reddish purplish tinge, forming a pleasing and attractive contrast with the green of other trees.

The Birch.—This tree in its varieties is adapted to poor soils. The *lenta* and *pubesceus* are the most common, while the *prunus padus* is one of the largest in growth and production of fruit. One dwarf variety *nana* makes a tree of only about five feet high. The varieties are admirable for crowning a point of rocky ledge or grouping with the Scotch Larch and Hemlock or White and Combined Pines.

Butternut—Juglaus Cineria.—Although not strictly to be classed among ornamental trees, yet the rapidity of growth while young, the habit of early bearing, together with the great value of its fruit, makes the Butternut a tree desirable to plant wherever a suitable place can be found.

Catalpa.—Syringafolia.—A native of our Southern States, the Catalpa or Shavasion is one of our most showy as well as rapid growing trees. It is not quite hardy in our Northern States, except where it has protection from evergreen trees. It is a tree that groups well with the Scotch, Austrian and yellow pines. A light, dry soil is best suited to its growth.

Cherry.—The Wild or Bird Cherry has several varieties popularly recognized, but only that classed by botanist as

Virginiana is desirable for parks or private grounds. The tree grows rapidly, and while its slender branches droop, its form is upright, spreading, and when in good soil attaining a large size. Like the birch graceful and pliant, swaying to every breeze its glossy foliage in the summer season, and its delicate, long, slender, purplish red spray in the winter, makes the Bird Cherry a very desirable tree for many situations. As a street tree it is unsuitable, and for small grounds it grows too large. Birds seem attracted to it, and nest in it perhaps more than in any other tree.

Perfumed or *Mahaleb Cherry.*—This variety makes a small, round-headed tree of fifteen to twenty feet in height, and the same in breadth. It is of great beauty and value as an ornamental tree. It has a strong, yet agreeable perfume when in flower, and bears an abundance of fruit. This fruit has its seeds and can be made profitable, as it is a variety upon which our large sweet cherries are worked as dwarfs, and the roots or plants of one year old are always in demand. Its abundant spray, pale green beads, which it holds until very late in autumn, makes for it a strong claim as a foreground trees whether evergreen or deciduous.

Double Flowering Cherry is a variety of the Heart Cherries, has a vigorous growth, and, in season, a profusion of double white flowers like miniature roses. It is a valuable tree for roadsides in the country, parks, or extensive private grounds.

Deciduous Cypress.—*Taxodium Distichia.*—Although a native of our Southern States, the Deciduous Cypress proves hardy in our Middle States and also a great portion of our Northern States. In foliage it is different from all other trees, with a resemblance to the Hemlock; it has a light, bright green, combined with an airy lightness of great elegance, pleasing and attractive to all. In low, wet grounds, as in its native habitat, it grows to a large tree, but planted in our common garden soils, it forms a tree of only medium height, say twenty to thirty feet. As it pushes its roots deep into the ground, it is always best to transplant young trees. Grouped with hemlocks and firs, its light green foliage and airiness contrast beautifully with the more sombre shades of evergreen.

*Dogwood—Cornus.—*The common Dogwood (*Cornus Florida*) abounds in all sections of the Middle States. It does not often grow over twenty feet high, but its profusion of white flowers in early spring have drawn the attention of ornamental planters to it, until it is now sought for and planted by every landscapist of any taste. As a small tree to skirt the boundaries of evergreen groups, peeping out from among them with its snowy flowers in spring, and its brilliant red berries and dark red foliage in autumn, few can equal it. There is a variegated leaved variety, its leaves blotched with white, that when the plant is to stand with other deciduous trees, is better because of the greater attractions created by its foliage, and there is also one, the *Sanguinea,* with its young shoots of a bright scarlet color, that is ornamental whether planted by itself or against a relief of evergreens.

Elm—From the abundance of Elms, everywhere native, over our country, and the almost perfect certainty of their living after transplanting with ordinary care, it has become one of our most popular street and park trees. Gracefully elegant, by reason of its long sweeping branches and its loose pendant, its tufted masses of foliage, vigorous and almost lofty in its growth, and adapting itself as it were to all soils, wet or dry, clay or sand, the American White Elm has no superior as a street or park tree—where it can be planted so as to give it room for development, but when planted, as it too often is, in small grounds or on the sides of narrow streets or avenues, where its limbs have to be lopped off or trimmed up, it is unsuited, because in so doing its beauty is destroyed and the owner has only a long bare trunk where he might have had, with some other variety, a mass of foliage and beauty. The Red Elm (*Feilea*) is more upright in its growth than the White and does not attain as great size, but it is not as desirable for planting in positions too confined for the White, as the European (*Camputris*) or Scotch (*Montana*) Elms. The European or English Elm forms a lofty tree of less spreading habit than our White Elm, and in retaining its foliage later extends, apparently, our season of summer. As a shade tree it is more compact and dense in its foliage, and therefore more suitable in the formation of masses or groups. A great number of varieties of this species are grown from seed, and the planter can frequently select a dozen trees of different habits among those offered by the dealer as one. Nurserymen offer over twenty-five as distinct varieties. A few of them are of due credit and value as novelties, viz.: The Purple-leaved, Slender Twigged, Gerroted-leaved and Cork Barked (*Suberosa*.) It is vigorous and hardy, foliage rich and dark, hanging late in autumn, and its branches and twigs covered with a fungous growth of a cork like substance, so singular and curious as to attract attention and admiration. The foliage of all the elms in autumn is of a yellow tint.

The Ginko—Salisburia.—A tree with foliage unlike any other. In form it has generally a neat, regular, open, conical head; its foliage on long petioles, giving it an airy and unique appearance that harmonizes well with buildings, but does not so well with masses or groups of other trees.

Horse Chestnut.—Esculus.—For bordering the lines of straight avenues and for public squares or town plots, where regularity and symmetry are desired rather than grandeur, for single lawn trees and for limited use in grouping with the Scotch and Austrian Pines, the Horse Chestnut is one of our best and most ornamental trees. The old white flowering has now given place to one of the same habit in growth, but producing double white flowers. Where the ground is limited, it is well to have the Variegated-leaved, Double Red Flowering and other rare and new varieties engrafted upon the Double White Flowering. The Dwarf Double Flowering (*Nana Fl. Pl.*) and of variety *Pavia*, the *Camea Superba*, *Camea Pubescens*, *Purpurea*, *Rubra*, *Flava*, etc., come into use along a line or as a group at a turn of the road. The growth of these is in no case of value, other than a low group of broad leaved shrubs.

Hickory.—Carya.—The difficulty of transplanting the Hickory or White Walnut has kept it from free use. The net of practice in the transplanting of this tree freely and safely is to dig a trench around a two years' seedling of one foot in depth, two feet diameter, and cut off every root, so that the whole can be raised like a ball. This course will make the hickory the next year as safe to transplant as any other tree.

Linden.—Tilia.—Under the name of Basswood our American Linden or Lime tree is well known. Of rapid growth, easily transplanted, full and flowing in its outline or form, its foliage broad and of a rich green, few of our native or exotic trees have more to recommend them than the Linden. It prefers and grows more vigorously in a light and rich deep soil, but grows well in even a poor sand or clay soil, provided it is not wet. Its regular, uniform, but flowing form, adapts it well to planting in grounds of the graceful school in composition, and also to avenues, streets and public parks. There are a number of varieties, the best of which, we think, is the *Alba* or White Leaved Linden, which has very broad foliage, deep green on the upper side and nearly white underneath, so that every breeze that rustles among it gives to it an airy and beautiful appearance. The European Linden has smaller leaves than our American, and is perhaps more regular in form, and there are varieties of it—one with the young shoots quite red and one with them yellow—that are extremely ornamental in winter, the red especially, when grouped with evergreens, forming conspicuous lines. There are also fancy varieties as the Fern-leaved, Grape-leaved, etc., that are curious and pretty, and may be worked on one of the Red Twigged European.

Locust.—Robinia.—We do not regard the Locust (*Var Robinia*) as of much value for planting on roadsides, in parks or private grounds. The best way to use the Spreading (*Horizontalis*), the Crisp-leaved (*Crispa*), the Rose Flowered (*Viscsa*), etc., is to graft them upon the Honey Locust (*Gleditschia Triacanthos*). This latter, the Honey Locust, is a tree that does not sucker, rarely if ever breaking under the strongest gales of wind, assumes to itself the privilege of growing in many shapes, from that of a tall, branching and lofty character, to one of almost horizontal form. In foliage it is light and open, feathery, and together with its wood studded with long, pointed thorns, and seed pods of five or six inches in length, which hang on all winter, create for it a tree very desirable in the composition of groups, and also for roadsides or streets, where only a partial, not deep shade is desirable.

Larch.—Larix—The European Larch is a tree almost indispensible in ornamental planting of grounds. Seemingly indifferent as to the nature of the soil, it grows with surprising rapidity in thin, poor, light sands, in wet, boggy loams, in high rocky knolls, or in rich garden loam. It should, however, be sparingly planted in grounds where the graceful, rather than the picturesque, is designed to be created. The European Larch, when the tree is so planted that it can plainly be seen, is very beautiful with its bright pink flowers early in spring.

Magnolia.—To this family, many varieties of which are the pride of our Southern States, too little attention is given by the majority of tree planters; whether it is that good plants are difficult to be obtained, or whether it is because the trees are rather sensitive and unwilling to be carelessly and negligently handled when transplanting, very few planters make room for them on their lists or in their grounds, but how any landscapist can form an extensive group of evergreens and deciduous trees without using Magnolias, is beyond our comprehension. In our experience we have found no difficulty when transplanting, provided we kept the roots from cold, drying winds or clear, burning suns; exposure to either of which, by reason of their soft, spongy texture, is injurious and often destructive of life. Of the varieties all are beautiful, but some are not perfectly hardy in the Northern States. A sandy, loamy soil suits them best, but if it is strictly dry the trees of some varieties, as *Macrophylla*, etc., when grown on their own roots, are liable to die out in from five to ten years. Any soil containing lime is injurious to the Magnolia. We prefer to make our soil, when not naturally suited, by digging a place three to four feet deep and eight to ten feet in diameter, and fill it with light, rich, fresh top soil drawn from the woods. The Magnolia *Acuminata*, or Cucumber Tree, as it is frequently called, is very upright and regular, almost cone-like in form, and for backgrounds or the center of groups one of the most desirable of all deciduous trees. It is the best of all as a stock to engraft any and all varieties upon it. The Magnolia *Macrophylla*, *Cordata*, *Auriculata*, *Conspicua*, *Soulangea*, *Longifolia*, *Gordoniana*, *Thompsoniana*, *Norbertiana*, *Speciosa*, *Superba*, *Lenna* and *Tripetela* are all superior when worked on the *Acuminata*. The *Glauca Purpurea* and *Gracilis* are of small growth on their own roots, and used mainly as the foreground of groups.

*Maple.—Acer.—*All the Maples are good as shade trees for lawn or roadside, but among them the *Rubrum*, Red Flowering, or, as generally termed, Scarlet Maple is most to be prized. Its red flowers and leaves in early spring or beginning of summer, its brilliant shades of red foliage in autumn, taken in connection with its rapid growth and upright, spreading form, render it one of the most ornamental of hardy trees. It may not be quite as rapid in growth as the Silver-leaved *(Dasycarpum)*, but is more upright and its branches less liable to be broken by heavy winds. The Silver-leaved is, however, a valuable variety, and where partially sheltered or where it can have an opportunity to develop itself, it is one of the most graceful as well as lofty of the species. As the trees are all grown from seeds, there is great variety of habit among them, some having almost as much of a drooping habit as the Willow, others of a spreading, open habit similar to American White Elm. For light sandy soils the Red and Silver-leaved are among the best, other varieties in light soils make little progress after a few years. The Sugar Maple *(Saccharinum)* makes one of the most compact and regular of round headed trees, forming a dense shade. It is, however, a a slow grower, and should be planted only in rich, deep, well drained soils. The Moosewood or Striped-barked Maple is a small growing variety, so also the *Campestris*, *Dissectum*, *Laciniata*, *Negundo Crispa.* The Sycamore Maple *(Pseudo Platanus)* is a stately, rapid growing tree, with broad foliage of a rich green. In the autumn its foliage becomes a rich golden yellow. The Norway Maple (*Platanoides*) is another desirable variety. It is often mistaken for the Sycamore Maple, but it is more upright, and does not make so large a tree. This with *Campestris* are admirably adapted to small grounds.

The *Macrophylla* or *Large Leaved* is one of the finest of upright growth and great beauty, and although introduced many years ago it is yet little known. There are numerous fancy varieties, such as Tricolor, Variegated-leaved, Cut-leaved, Purple-leaved, etc., all of which are curious and desirable in grounds of large extent, but in places where a limited number only can have place the Purple-leaved is the one particularly desirable. Its leaves are purplish underneath and pale green above when fully expanded, and at midsummer and thereafter until the fall of the leaves, every breeze that ruffles and disturbs them, produces a singular and pleasing effect in contrast with the foliage of other varieties. The Ash-leaved Maple or Box Elder (*Negundo Fraxinifolia*) is a **very** rapid growing **variety**, of great beauty from its peculiar formed leaves and its pale green, smooth young **wood.** It makes a large tree when grown in a deep, rich, moist soil, but in a light sandy loam or good garden soil, it forms **a** tree of medium size, which from its color of young wood in **winter is** exceedingly attractive and pleasing. It groups **admirably with** Pines.

Mulberry.—Morus.—Although not a tree of the highest type of beauty, **yet the** native Mulberry is not inelegant, and wherever it can be grown successfully, the great value of its fruit adds much to recommend its adoption in forming groups of deciduous trees, as it harmonizes well with the Linden, Catalpa, and some others of round heads and broad foliage. The variety now well known as Downing's Everbearing is a hardy as any, and its fruit is large and fine with the addition of blossoming and ripening a long time in succession. A rich, deep, loamy soil, well drained, suits it best, and in the northern sections of the Union it should be sheltered from severe winds and strong suns. In the Northern States it is unfitted for a street or park trees, but in the Southern and Middle States both the *Morus* and

Broussonetia are valuable trees for such uses.

Mountain Ash.—Pyrus.—Among professional as well as amateur planters, the European Mountain Ash is a deserved and general favorite. Its white flowers in the month of May, profusely spread out over its surface in thick, flat clusters, followed by bunches of round scarlet berries in autumn, and which if not destroyed or eaten by birds often hang on a great part of winter, making the tree highly ornamental when planted by itself, and still more so when it is the foreground of a cluster of Spruces or Pines. It does not grow of sufficient size for a street or park tree, but for small grounds, narrow roads and parks in cemeteries it is admirably adapted. It may be, and usually is, grown with a single stem with its branches thrown out at three or four feet from the ground, but on lawns or grass plots, and as connected with evergreens, it is much handsomer if permitted to throw out a number of stems directly from the crown. The American variety does not make quite as large a tree as the European, but it is more abundant in its flowers and fruits. The Sorb or Service tree *(Pyrus Domestica)*, and the White Beam *(Pyrus Vestita)*, the *Pyrus Hybrida*, and the *Pyrus Quercifolia*, with a number of dwarf and variegated foliaged varieties, are all of value.

Oak.—Quercus.—The Oak is a tree of song and tradition, but the difficulty of transplanting it after it has acquired a suitable size for position. Downing says of it that "to arrive at its highest perfection, ample space on every side must be allowed," and where such position can be given it in public or private grounds we should plant it; but in small suburban and village home grounds there are no such places, and their owners must be content with trees of a less historical or poetical interest. Of the varieties most ornamental, we enumerate the Rock Chestnut Oak *(Quercus Prinus Monticola)*, Chestnut White Oak *(Q. Prinus Palustris)*, the Yellow Oak *(Q. Prinus Acuminata)*, the Pin Oak *(Q. Palustris)*, the Willow Oak *(Q. Phellos)*, the Overcup White Oak *(Q. Macrocarpa)*, the Scarlet Oak *(Q. Coccinea)*, and English Oak *(Q. Robur)*. The Live Oak *(Q. Virens)* of the

South is beautiful and can be grown as a park tree, but it will not endure the climate of the Northern States. The Cork Oak (*Q. Suber*) is a very interesting and curious tree. If the proprietor of a place has a desire for Oaks, our advice is to prepare soil deep and rich, plant the acorns, staking around to prevent injury to the young plant.

Osage Orange.—Maclura.—This plant or tree is generally grown for the purpose of forming hedges, but when grown singly it makes a tree of medium size, with a regular round head, covered with clean glossy foliage and rich golden fruit, in appearance resembling the orange of commerce. It is admirably suited as a lawn tree for small plots and for grouping with other round headed deciduous trees of larger growth. In this latter position it should always be on the outside of the group. It is a tree well suited for planting on the narrow avenues of cemeteries, and for bold, rugged fronts of rocky banks. Upon lawns of large extent an elegant monster shrub tree can be created from the Osage Orange by annually heading it back near to the ground until it is induced to send up a dozen leading stems instead of one; these again, as they grow, want heading back from year to year, until the plant becomes a gigantic bush rather than a tree.

Poplar.—Populus.—Many of the Poplars are valuable trees in the decoration of scenery, but their use must be with moderation. They are all of rapid growth and easily transplanted. The Lombardy Poplar (*Populus Dilitata*) may often be introduced with great effect, and again, two or three trees of it planted directly in the rear of a building furnish a relief and background, adding greatly to appearance as a picture. When distant views are desired, permission to plant one or two Lombardy Poplars at or near the point will serve to attract the eye, and in themselves add an air of admiration to the scene. It should never be planted as a foreground tree. The Balsam Poplar (*Balsamifera*) and the Balm of Gilead Poplar (*Candicans*) very much resemble each other in their rapid growth and spreading habit, but their foliage is entirely distinct; the former having lanceolate oval leaves, while the latter has very large, broad, heart-shaped foliage, and is much the more desirable. Both are good for roadside trees or broad avenues, and their use in filling up low grounds or bordering streams of water is always satisfactory. As a background tree, covering and screening barns or other farm buildings, the Balm of Gilead is very effective. The Silver Poplar *(Abele)* is a tree remarkable for its silvery white underside of foliage. It was once pretty generally planted in lawns and groups, but its disposition to sucker makes it objectionable. As a tree to make conspicuous some particular high point, or where possible, to form the foreground of a group of dark firs, it is desirable and effective. All the Poplars bear the smoke and dust of cities with great indifference, and where pavements will serve to keep down the suckers, they are desirable because of their extremely rapid growth, exceeding perhaps that of any other tree.

Pepperidge.—Nyssa.—The Sour Gum or Pepperidge tree is generally, when wild, found growing in moist or wet land, but it will thrive in any good deep soil. The tree, from its dark green, glossy foliage in summer and the brilliant fiery tinge which it takes on when ripening its leaves, is extremely valuable for forming groups in the picturesque style. A single tree of it even, standing at some distance from the house and where its brilliant autumn tints can be readily seen, often forms for weeks a feature of beauty surpassing that of any other on the place.

Persimmon.—Diospyrus.—The Persimmon or Virginia Date Plum makes an open, irregular, half round-headed, rather erect tree of pleasing character and of medium size, that fits it well for grounds of limited extent. It groups well with the English Elm, the Bird Cherry and others, and when the value of its fruit is regarded, deserves a place in almost all grounds. In the southern sections of Illinois, Missouri, etc., there are varieties that ripen their fruits long before frosts, but the wild trees of its northern limits generally produce an austere fruit, quite uneatable until after being mellowed by frost. It is a good tree for planting in cemeteries, and for rocky positions where a light, airy character is desired to be retained.

LANDSCAPE GARDENING.   37

Paulownia.—Imperialis.—One of the finest of broad leaved trees, and in latitudes south of 41° it produces a profusion of purplish lilac flowers. North of 41° the tree is hardy, but the bloom is often destroyed by cold.

Sassafras.—Laurus.—Strange as it may seem this beautiful, fragrant, second-class growth of tree is rarely to be found in the nurseries, and he who wants it must go to the woods and dig for himself small plants. As an open foreground tree for groups, the glossy, deep green foliage of the Sassafras and its irregular swaying branches make it especially desirable.

Tulip Tree.—Liriodendron.—The Tulip or Whitewood is one of the most beautiful and stately of our native trees. It is a rapid grower, erect, yet partially spreading, forming a regular, even, conically round head, with a large, broad, rich, glossy leaf and smooth, clean bark. Like the Magnolias, its roots are soft and do not bear exposure to dry winds or sun when transplanting, and the planter must use care and attention in their removal. For avenues, for public or private parks, for single trees upon lawns, and especially for shade near the house, there is no tree its superior. In the month of June its profusion of large tulip-like flowers give it a richness and beauty all unlike that of any other tree, and to our view only equalled by some of the Magnolias. It requires a dry and deep rich soil in order to develop its greatest beauty, but it will thrive in any good loam where there is a perfect drainage.

Thorns.—Cratagus.—Of these second class trees, strictly shrubs, there are many varieties beautiful in flower and varied in foliage. They are of little value except when used in a hedge, and here unfortunately the pruning seems in a few years to destroy their vitality and they die out.

Walnut.—Juglans.—Under the name of Walnut we have the European Walnut and the Black Walnut of our forests. The European Walnut is not hardy in our Northern States. As an ornamental tree South it makes a pleasing variety, because of the contrast in its foliage with that of most other trees. The Black Walnut—*Juglans Nigra*—makes a very rapid growth and becomes a very large and spreading tree. It is unsuited to any but extensive grounds or farms.

Willow.—Salix.—There is a large variety of Willows, all of narrow leaves and slender branches or spray. Aside from the Weepers or Drooping, the Golden-barked is the only one of value.

ORNAMENTAL DECIDUOUS SHRUBS.

In all grounds a well appointed and arranged shrubbery is a most effective feature, and in grounds of small extent, such as the front gardens of suburban city lots, the use of shrubs or trees of small growth is more to be commended than those of a towering or large spreading habit. Just enough of large trees should be planted to form necessary shade, and then the effect and general impression of beauty be created by the planting of deciduous trees and evergreen shrubs. One of the most important things in planting shrubs is to attend particularly to the shades of green in foliage ; another is an understanding of soils in which they will grow and develop themselves most luxuriantly. Even the effect of perspective may be considerably increased by the proper arrangement of trees. Shrubs whose leaves are of a gray or bluish tint, when seen over or between shrubs of a yellowish or bright green, will seem thrown into the distance. Those, again, with small or tremulous leaves should be set over or before those with large, broad, fixed foliage. Where the situation will permit, three or five Lilacs, or Weigelas, or Tree Honey-suckles, or Japan Quince with Forsythias and Deutzia Scabra, as a foreground, may be grouped together.

"A shrubbery," says Mr. Phillips, "should be planted as a court or stage dress is ornamented, for general effect and not for particular and partial impression. Boldness of design, which seems to be more the offspring of Nature and chance than of art

LANDSCAPE GARDENING.   39

and study, should be attempted, but though boldness is what the planter should aspire to, all harshness or too great abruptness must be avoided by a judicious mixture of plants whose colors will blend easily with one another." The most beautiful of shrubs should of course be planted in the most conspicuous places, and the whole with respect to evergreens so arranged as to contribute in making bright the gloom of winter, in reducing and softening the glare of summer, and assist in lengthening the season by their early flowers in spring and their ripening berries in autumn.

CONDENSED DESCRIPTIONS OF ORNAMENTAL SHRUBS.

It is impossible for us to give full descriptions of all the ornamental shrubs within the limits of what we design to make a plain, cheap, practical work. We must therefore make short descriptions of the leading shrubs, free of botanical names, as follows:

The *Rose Acacia* is an old shrub, with rose colored flowers in July.

The *Althea* is a shrub from four to six feet in height, and should be trimmed every spring.

The *Alder* has varieties, but its beauty is only developed in low, damp grounds.

The *Almond* is a dwarf shrub, with flowers like double roses of varied colors.

The *Azalea* is known as the Swamp Pink or Swamp Honeysuckle, and is generally planted with Kalmias and Rhododendrons.

The *Amorpha* is a shrub with long spikes of blue or purple flowers. There are several varieties, but all like other shrubs need severe annual pruning.

The *Amelanchier*, or more generally known as Shad Bush, in early spring has white flowers covering the whole tree.

The *June Berry*, a variety of the above, with white flowers in pendulous racemes. A variety of this has wood of a dark red or blood color.

The *Barberry* has many varieties which may be grouped together with good effect.

The *Buckthorn* is one of the best of hedge plants, and quite ornamental when planted singly.

The *Buffalo Tree* is a sexual plant, ornamental, with silvery foliage. If a half dozen of the female plants surround the male, fruit is produced of value for tarts and exceedingly ornamental.

The *Bladder Senna* is a shrub of varied colors in its blossoms, with balloon-like pods that follow the flowers.

The *Bladder Nut* has a profusion of white bell shaped flowers early in summer.

The *Clethra* is an erect shrub, with spikes of white flowers from July to September.

The *Flowering Currant* has many varieties. Gordon's is the best.

The *Deutzia* is a low growing shrub of great beauty.

The *Golden Bell Shrub* has several varieties, all producing yellow bell-shaped flowers in spring.

The *Hydrangea* is generally of herbaceous character and requires protection in winter, but there are some new varieties of these that are exceedingly valuable.

The *Upright or Tree Honeysuckle* is one of the best flowering shrubs.

The *Kœlreuteria* is a second class tree, a little tender, but prominent as a novelty.

The *Laburnum* or Golden Chain is one of the most beautiful, when in flower, of the large shrubs.

The *Lilac*, known botanically as *Syringa Vulgaris*, is well-known. It has a tendency to sucker, but a little attention from year to year will enable the grower to keep it to a single stem, and grouped with the Snow-ball, Red Bud, Purple Fringe, it is of great beauty. Josikaea and Charles Xth have much the habit of the old variety, but flowers of a different color. The *Chinese* and *Persian* Lilacs are of a dwarf size, and suited to mingle with Spruces.

The *Mezereum* is a small shrub of about two feet in height, giving a profusion of pink or white flowers in early spring.

The *Double Flowering Plum*, like the Double Flowering Thorn, is a compact, round headed large shrub of great beauty when in bloom.

The *Purple Fringe* is one of the varieties of *Rhus*, of value and beauty. It is known as Smoke Tree, Jews Beard, etc.

The *Japan Quince* has many varieties in colors, from white to scarlet in its blooms. It will always find a place in all grounds, as it is a beauty in itself.

The *Red Bud* or Judas Tree forms a low, round headed tree, abounding in a profusion of pinkish red flowers in early spring, and when planted where Evergreens make the background, it is one of the valued second-class trees.

The *Stuartia* and *Snow Berry* are low shrubs of value.

The *Strawberry Tree* or Burning Bush is a variety of beauty in foliage and its fruit of a bright red, holding on nearly all winter.

The *Sophora* is a fine shrub south say of Philadelphia, north of that it is only half hardy.

The *Shrubby Spireas* are all of value and beauty for gardens or cemeteries. The following are, according to the botanical terms, among the best, viz.: *Prunifolia Flore Pleno, Niconderti, Thalactoides, Crenatu, Lanceolata Flore Plena, Callosa Alba* and *Floribunda* all have white flowers. The *Bella, Nobleana, Eximia, Callosa, Douglassii* and *Billardii* all have pink or rosy flowers.

The *Snow Drop*, botanically *Halesia*, is one of the most beautiful of shrub trees. There are two varieties, a four-winged and a two-winged, in flower. Their best position is as a foreground of a group of Evergreens.

The *Sweet Scented Shrub* is of low growth, with dark wood and foliage, a chocolate colored flower highly perfumed.

The *Syringa*, or Mock Orange, is a well known old shrub of varieties, among which the Garland, Gordons and Profuse Flowering are among the best. There are some dwarf varieties.

The *Tamarisk* is one of the most delicate and airy like in appearance among shrubs. The African and Algiers are among the hardiest.

The *Weigela*.—Among all the hardy flowering shrubs, introduced within the past thirty years, this, as a class, takes a first rank. It is of easy cultivation, suited to all soils. It bears pruning freely, and may be grown as a bush or to a single stem.

The *White Fringe Tree*, or Virginia Snow Flower, is a shrub or low tree, doing best in moist soil, producing a profusion of drooping white flowers in early summer.

PLAN No. 1.

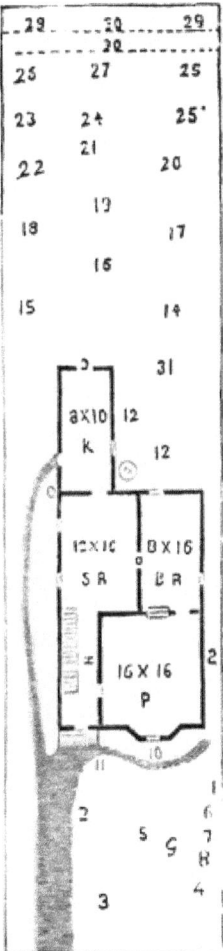

This plan is for a lot 30 by 150 feet and on a scale of 25 feet to the inch. The house, as a main, is 20 by 32 feet, and placed 2 feet from the boundary line on one side and 8 feet from the line on the other side. The position of the rooms are shown, also the chimney, which could have three separate flues for fires from three rooms. The hall and stairs are shown, and the 16 feet long building in rear is supposed to be used as a wood shed and washing room. The well, marked with an o, is on the side where driving may come, while the cistern, marked o, is where water can be taken into three rooms.

The pathway to the door is shown on the plan, and all the front aside from this, as well as the wide space from the front to rear of wood shed, should be kept in grass.

Hedges of the various Evergreens, such as the Hemlock, Norway Spruce, Arbor Vitæ, etc., may be planted, if desired, on each of the lines of boundary and in front, except where the entrance way is, but they should be kept yearly and properly pruned. When the trees are planted they should be mulched with litter, tan bark, etc., say two feet in diameter from the body.

The following numbers, with the names of trees, etc., all attached, correspond with their places for growth on the map:

1—Cembrian Pine.
2—Magnolia Glauca.
3—American White Spruce.
4—Austrian Pine.
5—Dwarf Horse Chestnut.
6—Magnolia Purpurea.
7—Strawberry Tree.
8—Purple Fringe.
9—Japan Quince.

10—This is designed for a bud of flowers of sorts, Lilacs, Geraniums, Tea Roses, Bourbon Roses, Lantanas, Verbenas, etc., such as may please the taste of the owner and yet be in bloom most of the season. A good effect is to raise the rear of the bed next the house to the upper tier of the underpinning, then make it a rolling grade down to the turf. Then place here and there a broken stone of varied color, filling in and around them with good soil from the woods, and then plant the American Ivy or Virginia Creeper, varieties of Hardy Clematis and Trailing Junipers for the purpose of keeping a green show in winter.

11—Tom Thumb, or some other dwarf sort of Arbor Vitæ.
12, 12—Two varieties of Apples, grown as dwarfs.
13—Red Jacket Cherry.
14—Rockport Cherry.
15—Early Richmond Cherry.
16—Black Tartarian Cherry.
17—Early York Peach.
18—Old Mixon Free Peach.
19—Crawford's Early Peach.
20 to 25—Varieties of Dwarf Pears as follows:
  1 Beurré Giffart.   1 Bartlett.
  1 Duchess d'Angoulême. 1 Tyson.
      1 Beurré d'Anjou.
26, 27 and 28—Grapes:
  1 Concord.   1 Delaware.
    1 Hartford Prolific.
29, 29—Quinces.
30,30—Rows for Currants or other small fruits

PLAN No. 2.

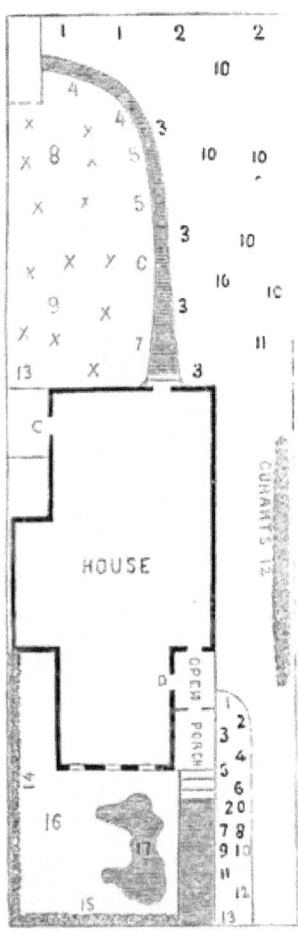

This plan is made only to show how a place may be improved. Scale 25 feet to the inch. The house being already built and fronting 20 feet back from the street line, one side is so near the adjoining line that the drip of the eaves really falls upon other property, while on the other side there is but just good room for a carriage or cartway, for delivery of coal, etc., say 12 feet. The distance in the rear of the house is near 50 feet, with little or nothing now upon it but an outhouse or privy. We commence the improvement of this plan from the rear, and shall give a fair estimate of the cost.

In this, as in all planting, our advice is never to buy large, tall trees, but take stocky, well branched ones, three to five feet in height.

1, 1—Quinces.
2, 2—Dwarf Apples trees or varieties:
    1 Red Astrachan.
    1 Duchess of Oldenburgh.
3, 3, 3, 3—4 Concord Grape Vines on trellis or stakes No arbor.
4, 4—2 Hartford Prolific Grapes.
5, 5—2 Delaware Grapes.
6—1 Martha.
7—1 Telegraph. All the Grapes to be trained on wires or stakes.
8—Early Richmond Cherry.
9—Rockport Cherry.
10—Six Dwarf Pears, as follows:
    1 Beurre Giffart.
    1 Duchess d'Angouleme.
    1 Louise Bonne de Jersey.
    1 Bartlett.
    1 Rostiezer.
    1 Beurre d'Anjou.
11—Black Tartarian Cherry.
12—Row of Currants.
13—Red Jacket Cherry.
X—This cross indicates places for Gooseberry Bushes.

Estimates of value of good trees for this planting at regular retail rates of the best nurserymen:

2 Apple or Orange Quince	$ 1.00
2 Dwarf Apples	.60
10 Grape Vines	5.00
4 Cherries	2.00
6 Dwarf Pears	3.00
12 Currants	2.00
12 Gooseberries	2.00
	$15.60

Doubtless from 10 to 20 per cent. less would fill this order, if given to a responsible Nurseryman.

Labor of planting	3.00
Total	$18.00

Now we will take the arrangements of the foreground.

No. 20 is designed for planting of hardy flowering shrubs, and the numbers in this block have no reference to the rear of the house, but each has the name of the plants to be there placed:

1—Red-fruited Berberry.
2—Euonymous or Strawberry Tree.
3—Weigela Rosea.
4—Variegated Wiegela.
5—Wiegela Amabilis.
6—Gordon's Syringa.
7—Spirea Lanccolata fl. plena.
8—Spirea Reveesii Cobusta.
9—Deutzia Crenata, flora plena.
10—Magnolia Rubra.
11—Deutzia Gracilis.
12—Hydrangea Paniculata Grandiflora.
13—Variegated-leaved Dogwood.
14—Hedge of Norway Spruces.
15—Along this front line have it raised a foot or more higher than the sidewalk, and with a rolling bank. Then gather rough boulders, broken stones of color, lay them along, two and three in one place and five in another, with here and there a single one. Arrange it so that they shall not be on a level, but a broken line. Now fill in among the stones along the line with creeping hardy vines, both Evergreen and Summer Flowering, being careful to have some of the Ampelopsis or Virginia Creeper, the Wistaria and Clematis Virginica. Use the best of light rich loam for the planting of the vines along the line. It would also improve their growth were the ground along the line deeply dug and richly manured before placing the stones and plants.
16—Purple-leaved Maple.
17—Bed for flowering plants, such as Roses, Geraniums, Lantanas, Lilies, Heliotrope, Caleus, Verbenas, Sweet Alysum, Tuberoses, Salvias, etc.

Should this property change hands and the coming man wish to have a barn and keep his own carriage and horses, the entrance road now proposed to be kept in grass might be graded, and position for the barn be made by simply removing some dwarf pears,—a tree that can at any age be transplanted successfully.

PLAN No. 3.

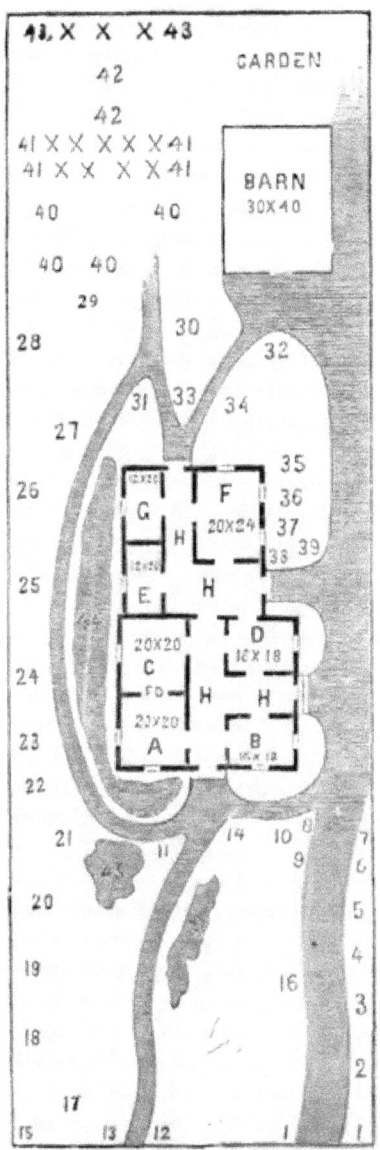

This is designed for a gentleman's suburban residence, and embraces 100 feet front upon the street with 300 feet in depth of lot.

The ground plan of the house is our own, and the structure of it we design to be of a plain substantial structure, with no attempt at Italian, Doric, Norman, Gothic Grecian or any other specific, distinct order. Taking the ground plan as presented, it will be seen that we have not made it to work from, for we have not shown how closets and shelves can be made and incorporated in the walls without disfiguring the rooms and adding greatly to the expense of construction. We design it to have a basement for coal, etc., and to be two stories high, with a Mansard roof as an attic, and we advise whoever may build from suggestions herein, to have a "Porte Cochen" or covered archway, for the getting in and out of the carriage. We have made no provision for the bath room on the first floor, believing that should be on the sleeping or second floor.

The numbers given in this schedule of explanation have each the variety or tree plant, and correspond with the numbers on the plan.

The scale of the drawing or design is 50 feet to the inch:

1. 1—Purple leaved Maples.
2—Curled Ash-leaved Maple.
3—Crested-leaved Beech.
4—Fern-leaved Beech.
5—Dwarf Birch.
6—Cut-leaved Alder.
7—Dwarf Hybrid Mountain Ash.
8—Norway Spruce (*Var Excelsa Pygmea.*)
9—Norway Spruce (*Var Excelsa Mucronata.*)
10—Norway Spruce (*Var Tortuosa Compacta.*)
11—Hemlock Dwarf (*Var Canadensis Nana.*)
12—Purple-leaved Beech.
13—Purple-leaved Elm.
14—Tom Thumb Arbor Vitæ.
15—Tulip Tree.
16—Weeping Birch (*Var Elegans Pendula.*)
17—Magnolia Soulangeana.
18—White Double Flowering Horse Chestnut.
19—Magnolia Glauca.
20—White-leaved Linden.
21—Ash-leaved Maple.
22—Lobels Maple.
23—Cembrian Pine.
24—Cut-leaved Weeping Birch.
25—White or Weymouth Pine.
26—Nordmann's Silver Fir.
27—Hemlock.
28—Austrian Pine.
29—Magnolia Acuminata.
30—Norway Spruce.
31—Imperial Cut-leaved Alder.
32—Scotch Pine.
33—Purple-leaved Berberry.
34—Norway Spruce.
35—American Silver Fir.
36—Siberian Arbor Vitæ.
37—Pinus Pumila.
38—Pinus Mugho Rotundata.
39—Pinus Mugho.
40—Varieties of Sweet Cherries:
   Black Tartarian.   Rockport.
   Red Jacket.   Elton.
      Early Purple Guigne.
41—Dwarf Pears of varieties:
   Beurre Giffart.   Bartlett.
   Clapp's Favorite.   Rostiezer.
   Belle Lucrative.   Tyson.
   Duchess d'Angouleme.   Howell.
   Louise Bonne de Jersey.   Sheldon.
   Conseiller de la Cour.   Beurre d'Anjou.
      Doyenne du Comice.
42—Rows of Grapes.
43—Dwarf Apples.

The varieties to fill these two last fruits is left to please the taste of the planter or owner of the land.

44—This bed is designed to be filled with hardy flowering shrubs, from the front corner of the house back. Place the tallest and strongest growers at the back end and so along the line next the house, then tone down toward the path with those of more slender growth; and in trimming yearly, cut so as to keep a rolling line from the house to the path, all the time keeping the rear end the highest. That portion of this bed we should plant with Tulips, Lilies, Hyacinths and Crocus, and in summer, after the early flowers are gone, put in Tuberoses, Verbenas, or any other small plants that must die or be taken out in autumn, when the bed wants a mulch covering of good leafy loam.

45—This bed may be planted partly with herbaceous Peonies, and then the Sweet Peas, Lantanas and many other summer flowering plants may be worked in for the late season.

46—Is a bed for Roses, Geraniums and any other free blooming and beautiful flowering plants the owner may choose. In the autumn it may be filled with any small and cheap plants of Evergreens to keep free from view the bare ground. The surrounding of the roots of the trees, say four feet in diameter, should have a mulch of some kind for two or three years, and then all but the flowering shrubbery beds and fruit garden may be kept in turf.

PLAN No. 4.

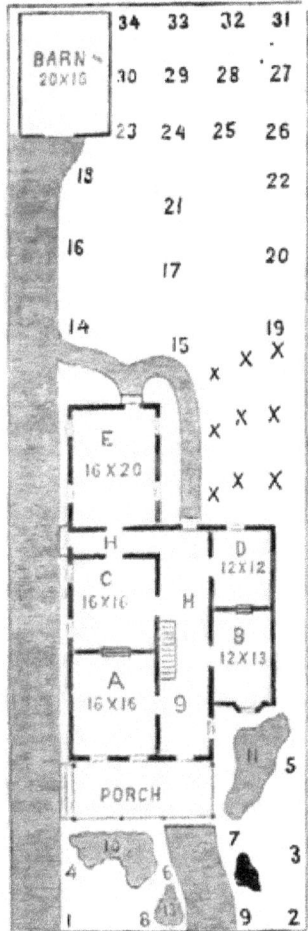

SCALE, 30 FEET TO ONE INCH.

This plan is for a lot 50 by 150 feet. The main of the house is 36 by 24 feet, two stories high, with a wing of one story, 12 by 28 feet. and a kitchen of 16 by 20 feet in the rear of the main building. The height of stories may and must be governed by the builder. We suggest. however, that the lower story be twelve feet high and the upper eight feet. The kitchen may be carried up with the main building. and if widened to its width would make a good wash room and also a storage room. The main hall could be let into it four feet, and then a side door connecting with a path outside, as here shown, only spread out to meet the spread of the building. The porch in front of the main building is 8 feet, and its style must correspond with the balance of the building. A bay window is placed to light the front room in the wing, and the chimneys marked, except the kitchen, where a brick flue will be needed from first ceiling. The barn we have calculated only for a single horse and buggy, but it, of course, can be enlarged.

In the planting of the grounds the numbers on the plan correspond with the following schedule list. In this we have not calculated for vegetable growing, believing fruit to be more profitable and more difficult to purchase than vegetables.

The drive or carriage way shows a landing at the porch, and then again at the side hall door.

In the planting of this design we have only given the front as the decorative portion, giving all the balance to such fruits as it is difficult to purchase in good order at reasonable rates. At the same time we have tried to include some that we count as better gathered from the vine or plant than those of the same in market:

1—Purple-leaved Maple.
2—Purple-leaved Elm.
3—Indian Birch (*Bhojputtra*.)
4—Cut-leaved Weeping Birch.
5—Oak-leaved Mountain Ash.
6—Birch.—Variety, *Elegans Pendula*.
7—Tom Thumb Arbor Vitæ.
8—Pinus Pumilo.
9—Norway Spruce (*Var Tortuosa Compacta*.)
10—This bed, (the form of which is outlined,) should be planted with Lilies, Tulips, Hyacinths and other bulbs for early spring blooming; then afterwards fill in with Verbenas, Geraniums, Sedums, Ivies, and various annuals, such as Balsams, Sweet Peas, Mignonette, Alyssum, etc. At each post of the porch there should be planted a climbing plant. The following are four valuable hardy varieties, viz.: American Ivy or Virginia Creeper, Clematis *Virginiana*, *Periploca Graca* or Virginia Silk, Wistaria.
11—This bed should be planted with hardy, low growing, flow. ring shrubs, such as the Berberry, Calycanthus, Corchorus, Gordon's Flowering Currants, Dentzias of varieties, Forsythia, Hydrangea Paniculata, Persian or Chinese Dwarf Lilacs, Purple Flowering Magnolia, Spireas, and one or two of Weigelas'. The distance apart in planting should be two to two and one-half feet, and each year the plants should be pruned back from half to two-thirds of the year's growth.
12—This bed should have Crocus and Narcissus bulbs for early spring blooms, then be filled with Geraniums and Tuberoses intermixed.

13—This bed should be filled with perpetual blooming roses of varieties. It should be dug very deep, at least two feet, and filled in, as a mixture with the earth, with decomposed or old rotten manure. The plants may be set eighteen inches to two feet apart.
14—Rockport Cherry.
15—Black Tartarian Cherry.
16—Red Jacket Cherry.
17—Elton Cherry.
18—Early Richmond or Louis Phillip Cherry.
19—Early York Peach.
20—Old Mixon Freestone Peach.
21—Crawford's Early Peach.
22—Ward's Late Freestone Peach.
23 to 30—Dwarf Pears as follows, viz.:
  Beurre Giffart.   Bartlett.
  Duchesse d'Angouleme.   Tyson.
  Beurre d'Anjou.   Beurre Diel.
  Louise Bonne de Jersey.
31 to 34—Dwarf Apples as follows:
  Red Astrachan.   Gravenstein.
  Large Sweet Bough.   Fameuse.
X, X—The rows with crosses drawn over the lines are for grapes, the Concord, Hartford Prolific, Telegraph and Martha, each planted 8 feet apart in the row. Delaware, Iona, Mottled, Croton, Lydia and Rebecca may be planted 6 feet apart in the rows.

PLAN No. 5.

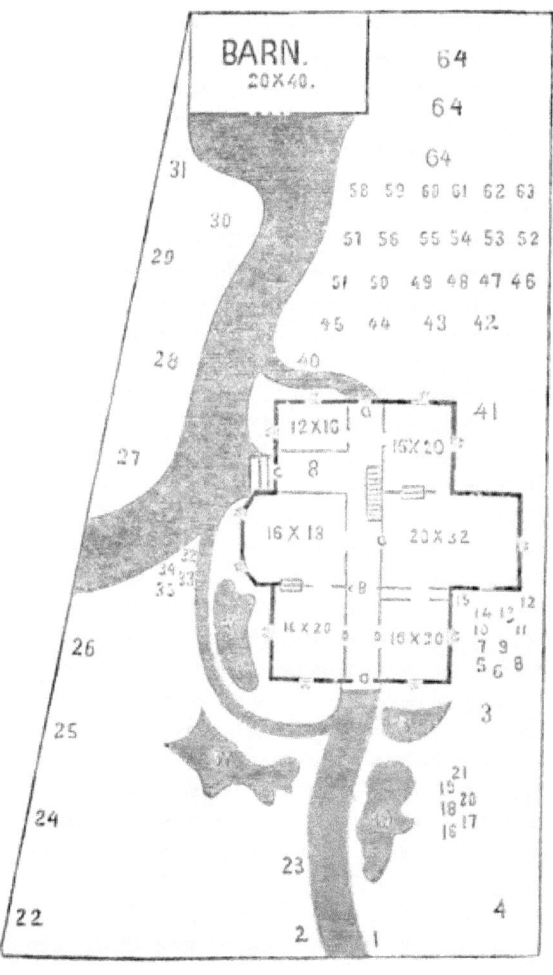

Scale, 40 feet to one inch.

This plan is made to fit a corner lot where the streets do not run at right angles with each other. The front is supposed to be upon the main travelled street, and is 100 feet. The side street, where we enter by carriage, may be new and as yet little built upon, but time makes many changes. The depth of the lot is supposed to be 200 feet, and while the ground plan of the house shows the size and position of the rooms, no porch or "Porte Cochen" has been planned, but any good architect can add it, according to the style of architecture. In planning the house, we have looked forward to the builder making it two stories high, with a basement or cellar for storage. The barn, 20 by 40 feet, we leave for whoever uses this to arrange according to his wants.

As with all of the other plans the figures on the ground correspond with this schedule, of what to plant and where:

1—Cut-leaved Beech.
2—Slender Twigged Elm (*Var. Campestris Viminalis.*)
3—Purple-leaved Maple.
4—Red Flowering Horse Chestnut.
5—Deutzia Crenata, flore pleno.
6—Deutzia Gracilis.
7—Persian White Lilac.
8—Magnolia *Oborata.*
9—Hydrangea *Paniculata Grandiflora.*
10—Dwarf White Horse Chestnut. (*Paria Macrostachya.*
11—Scarlet Japan Quince.
12—Euonymus or Strawberry Tree.
13—Gordon's Flowering Currant.
14—Pink Flowering Upright Honeysuckle.
15—Desbois' Weigela.
16—Spirea Eximea.
17—Weigela (*Var Hortensis Nivea.*)
18—Spirea Douglassii.
19—Spirea Prunifolia, flore pleno.
20—Pink Flowering Upright Honeysuckle. (*Var Pulverulenta.*)
21—Calycanthus, or Sweet Scented Shrub.
22—Norway Spruce, of a drooping character.
23—Weeping Birch (*B. Elegans Pendula.*)
24—Magnolia Soulangiana.
25—*Salisburia Adiantifolia.*
26—White-leaved Linden.
27—Rockport Cherry.
28—Elton Cherry.
29—Black Tartarian Cherry.
30—Red Jacket Cherry.
31—American White Spruce.
32—Pinus Mugho.
33—Tom Thumb Arbor Vitæ.
34—Norway Spruce (*Var Excelsa Inverta.*)
35—Pinus Pumi io.
36—This bed (shown in outline) should be planted with hardy bulbs for spring blooming, and on their decay, annual flowers of varieties, Verbenas, etc., may take their place for balance of the season.
37—This bed is to be filled with varieties of perpetual roses.
38—This bed to be planted with Heliotropes, Geraniums, Tuberoses, etc., intermingled.
39—Plant this bed with Herbaceous Peonias, Phloxes, Campanulas, Dicentra, Iris, Liatris, Spireas and other hardy herbaceous plants.
40—Austrian Pine.
41—Early Richmond or Louis Phillipe Cherry
42 to 45—Dwarf Apples of variety.
46 to 63—Dwarf Pears of varieties, eight feet apart each way.
64—Rows for Grapes, eight feet apart each way.

PLAN No. 6.

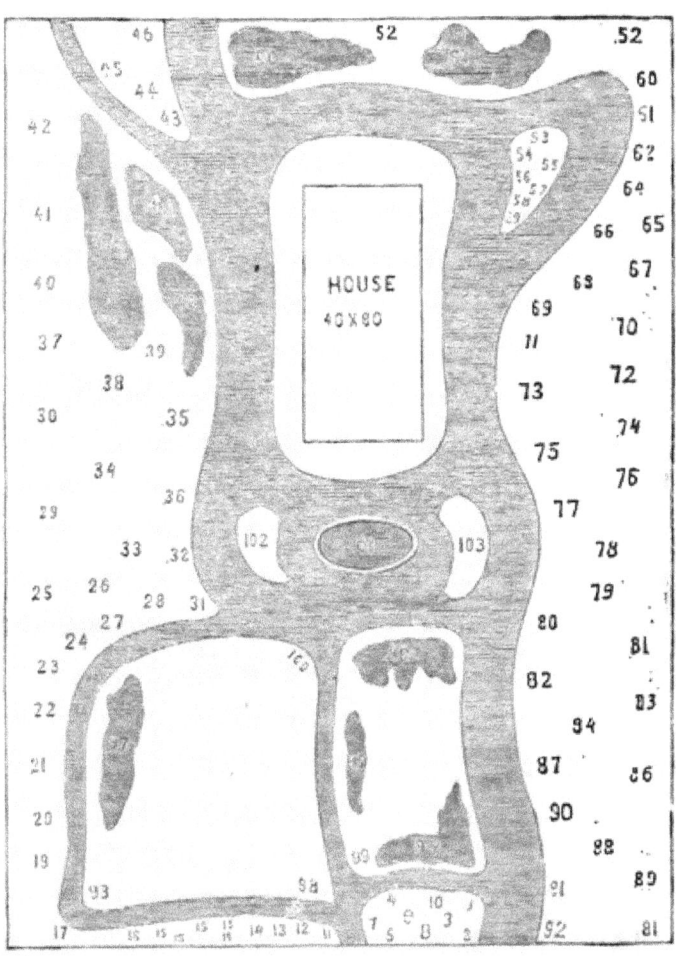

SCALE, 60 FEET TO ONE INCH.

In this we only show the arrangement of the foregrounds to the rear of the house. We have made no plan for the building, but have left 40 by 80 feet for its base, and have so planned the drive ways that it can be entered from any side.

The plan may be used for level ground, but often there is a rise of ground between the front and rear of the lot, and often this rise obstructs a fine rear view from the front lawn, unless it is graded to meet the level of the lawn upon the side where there is the most space. Should any one adopt this plan, having rising grounds on the position of the house, then we should advise him to grade only so as to make his drive ways level and easy of travel.

We have designed this for any place varying from 5 to 500 acres, giving the width of front 200 feet and the position of the house back from the main road 165 feet.

We have made no note of fruit trees in the planting, for few, if any, can be judiciously and tastefully mingled with the strictly ornamental.

The numbers on the plan correspond with the numbers given in the following schedule, and to each number we designate the name of the plant or tree, or give the class as a group.

We commence with the immediate front. All the space between the house and roads should be kept in clean turf. A hedge of Norway Spruce or Arbor Vitæ may be planted on each of the side borders of the lot here designed:

1—Hedge of Hemlock.
2—Pavia Carnea Superba.
3—Pavia Carnea Pubescens.
4—Pavia Purpurea.
5—Pavia Rubra.
6—Pavia Rubra Atrosanguinea.
7—Pavia Flava.
8—Trefoil Tree.
9—Sumach (*Var Glabra Laciniata.*)
10—Sumach (*Var Osbeckii.*)
11—Prunus Triloba.
12—Double Flowering Sloe Plum.
13—Halesia Tetraptera.
14—Euonymus or Strawberry Tree.
15—Five varieties of Amorpha or Bastard Indigo.
16—Cornus or Dogwood (*Var Mascula.*)
17—Purple-leaved Maple.
18—Purple-leaved Maple.
19—Mountain Ash.
20—Weeping Linden.
21—Weeping Beech.
22—Cut-leaved Weeping Birch.
23—Weeping Poplar.
24—Weeping Mountain Ash.
25—Camperdown Weeping Elm.
26—Cork-barked Weeping Elm.
27—Dwarf Weeping Cherry (*Pumila.*)
28—Ever-flowering Weeping Cherry (*Var Semperflorens.*)
29—European Weeping Ash.
30—Gold-barked Weeping Ash.

LANDSCAPE GARDENING.

31—Weeping Birch. Var *Elegans Pendula*.
32—Weeping Euonymous, Var *Pendula*.
33—Variegated Weeping Thorn.
34—Weeping Honey Locust, **Var.** *Bujoti Pendula*.
35—Weeping Larch.
36—American Weeping Willow.
37—Weeping Scotch Elm, Var. *Montana Pendula*.
38—Young's New Weeping Birch.
39—Small-leaved Weeping Elm, Var. *Microphylla Pendula*.
40—Magnolia **Acuminata.**
41—Tulip Tree.
42—European Sycamore Maple.
43—Swedish Juniper.
44—American Spruce.
45—Austrian Pine.
46—Norway Spruce.
47—Collection of Weigelas, planted three feet each way, within the form of the outlined bed.
48—Collection of Lilacs, two to three feet apart each way, according to habit of growth.
49—Collection of Spireas and Deutzias, planted from two to three feet apart, according to habit of growth.
50—Herbaceous Peonias in varieties, planted two feet apart.
51—Tree **Peonias**, varieties from 2½ to 3 feet apart each.
52, 52—Norway Spruces.
53—Staphylea or Bladder Nut.
54—Purple Fringe.
55—Gordon's Syringa.
56—Large Flowered Syringa.
57—Hoary-leaved Syringa.
58—White Fringe Tree.
59—High or Bush Cranberry, Var. *Oxycoccus*.
60—Snow Ball, *Viburnum Opulus*.
61—Snow Ball, Var *Anglicum*.
62—Snow Ball, Var *Pyrifolium*.
63—Snow Ball, Var *Raposum*.
64—Snow Ball, Var *Prunifolium*.
65—Snow Ball, Var *Lantauoides*.
66—Snow Ball, Var *Plicatum*.
67—American Arbor Vitæ.
68—Corsican or Norway Pine.
69—Austrian **Pine.**
70—White Pine.
71—Cembrian Pine.
72—Scotch Pine.
73—Red Bird or Judas Tree.
74—American White Spruce, *Abies Alba*.
75—American Red Spruce, *Abies Rubra*.
76—Dwarf White Pine, *Strobus Nana*.
77—Balsam Fir.
78—Lawson's Cypress.
79—Hemlock.
80—Banksian Pine.
81—European Silver Fir.
82—Nootka Sound **Cypress** or **Thujopsis** Borealis.
83—Siberian **Arbor** Vitæ.
84—Arbor Vitæ, **Var** *Gigantea*.
85—Arbor Vitæ, Var *Globosa*.
86—Salisburia Adiantifolia.
87—Oak-leaved Mountain Ash.
88—Double-flowering White Horse Chestnut.
89—English Elm.
90—Serrated-leaved Elm.
91—Slender Twigged Elm.
92—Elm, Var *Stricta Oxoniense*.
93—Magnolia Glauca.
94—Plant this bed with Hybrid Perpetual Roses of varieties. Dig the ground deep, and make it rich.
95—**This bed is for** Geraniums, Heliotropes, etc., **etc.**
96—**Make this bed deep and rich. Plant in it** Japan **Lilies, Tulips, Hyacinths, etc., and as the spring blooms fade, put in Verbenas or any free blooming, tender plant.**
97—**In this bed mingle Tea and Bourbon Roses with varieties of the rare and beautiful Clematis.**
98—Imperial Cut-leaved Alder.
99—Tom Thumb Arbor Vitæ.
100—Chinese Golden Arbor Vitæ. **Variety** *Aurea.*
101—Oval bed in front of house. The outer line, marked *a*, **should be** planted with *Juniperus Repens*, once in three feet and **one foot back of** the edge all around the oval. The center of this **bed should** be raised one foot above the edge. The **next** planting should be inside of the above two feet **of** *Juniperus Nana*, one in two feet. Next inside plant *Juniperus Squamata*, same as others. In the center of this oval plant one *Abies Excelsa Pygmea*, and at each end plant an *Abies Tortuosa Compacta*, then fill the remaining space with *Abies Nigra Pumila*.
102—If the planter resides where the Yew is hardy, plant this bed with varieties of that Evergreen shrub. If the Yew is not hardy, then fill this bed **with plants of** the Dwarf Hemlock variety, *Abies Canadensis Nana*.
103—In this bed place the Dwarf White Pine. —*Pinus Strobus Nana*—In **the center**, three plants on the long line three **feet** apart; then plant the *Pinus Mugho Rotundata*, say three plants, and make up the balance with *Pinus Mugho*.

Landscape or Home Adornment.

Dipping into my portfolio a few days since, and looking over sketches of plans that I had made for various gardens, it occurred to me that perhaps some of these skeleton plans might be of use in communicating ideas for working up some new place about to be created by a reader of rural art, and therefore I have transcribed and here offer two of them.

As the style of the house, architecturally, as well as the association of the neighboring lots, has much to do with the kind of trees to be planted, I have omitted any detail, because such detail would be of little or no avail. I will merely say that if the house is a square character, with a flat roof and standing on nearly level land, then the prevailing character of the trees should be of a round-headed habit; but if the house is of a pointed gothic, or with many broken yet harmonious lines, and its location on some elevated position, then spiral and pointed trees should be largely introduced, and especially near the house.

This was designed for a lot the elevation of which at the house is some six feet or more above the grade at the public street, and the house situated about two hundred and fifty feet back therefrom.

The owner of this desired as few paths and roads as could be, and meet the actual daily travel demand. Neither did he want provision for many flower-beds, as he only kept one man to care for horses, garden and all work. The beds next the public road are designed to be planted with flowering shrubs, in order to break a little the lawn from open exposure. So the bed on the right of entrance footpath is to be planted with shrubs, and also that where the carriage-road comes near the boundary to the left.

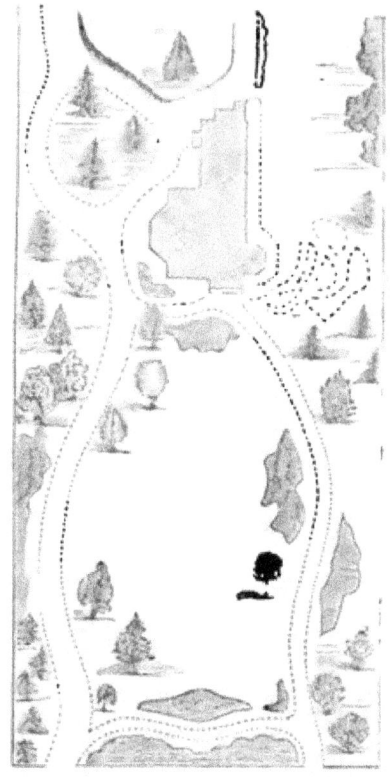

The beds near the house in front are filled with low trailing Evergreens, as Daphne Cneorum, Juniperus Squamata, Repens, etc., while the bed on the left of the footpath is planted with hardy Perpetual Roses and tree Peonias, keeping the flower-garden proper up near the house and immediately in view of the drawing-room bay window. As most of the landing is at the rear hall door, the turn-way is thrown in there, and a hedge borders the road on one side, separating it from the fruit or vegetable garden, barn, etc., beyond.

The foregoing was designed worked out, written upon and published some years since, but as the generality of the plan has met favor with many of those who have employed me in my profession, I decide to include it in this work.

The illustrations of trees in the plan will give to any sensible man an idea of what they are, while the text above tells of where to plant flowering shrubs, and of course the flower garden will be changed almost yearly by those who reside upon the place.

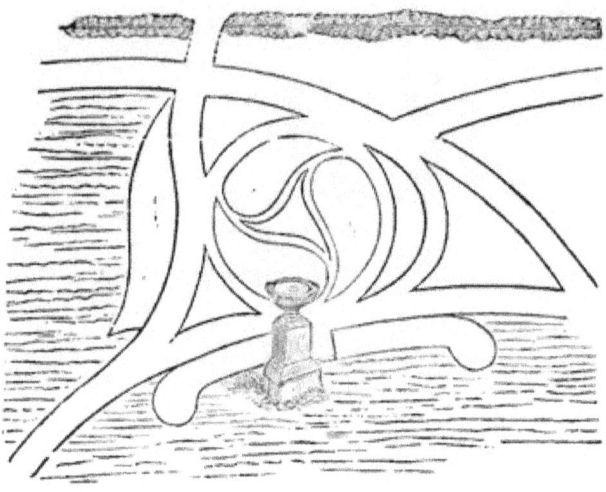

Fig. 8.—Walks, etc.—Ground Plan.

For a plot with parallel boundary lines, the accompanying design (fig. 8) is one of the simplest and yet most effective which I have ever seen. By examining, it will be observed that the center is a simple circle from which four beds are formed, and from outside of that the paths and beds are made to accommodate natural lines of travel, which the position of the house, being on the side where stands the vase, and the opening in the opposite hedge seems to demand. Planting these separate beds with masses of flowers, each of a distinct color, produces a constant feature of interest and attraction. The shaded line is a hedge, having a passway to visit the next occupant of a lot.

Fig. 9.—View of Grounds.

Fig. 9 shows what we have done around an irregular formed artificial pond in six years from planting.

Fig. 10.—Fountain.

As I have said that a fountain may be had at a little cost beyond that of the pipes and their laying, and at the same time be made to harmonize with tree and surrounding, I offer the illustration, fig. 10, which is simply varied pieces of rock laid up around the center pipe, and having a wire-work frame, into the meshes of which are woven various colored stones as the basin or urn. A circular pipe surrounds it, over which is laid a pavement of stone in mosaic work, and from between which numerous smaller jets of water arise. In the plinth of the structure, amid the rocks, ferns and water-plants are planted. The mosaic pavement is level with the surrounding turf, with just sufficient dip toward the center to draw the waste water, which passes off by means of a pipe beneath.

PLAN No. 9.

SCALE, 40 FEET TO ONE INCH.—LOT 100 BY 200 FEET.

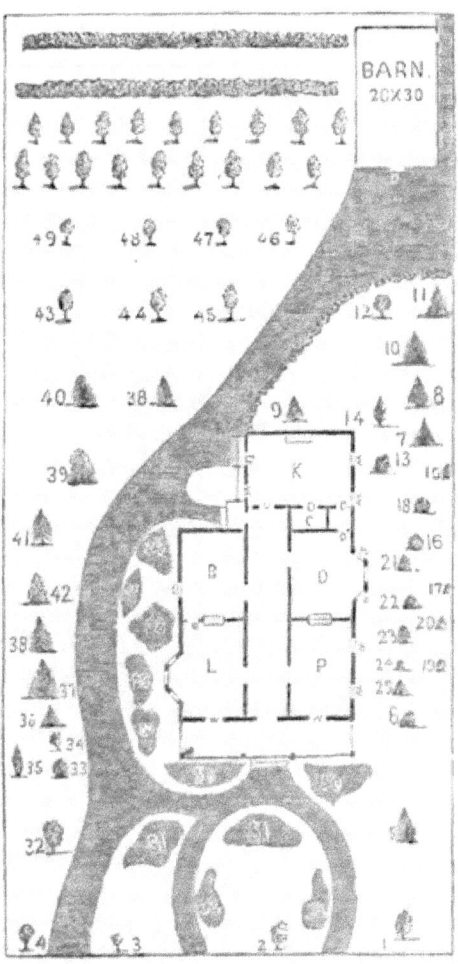

Plan 9 is for a lot 100 by 200 feet. The scale on which it is drawn is 40 feet to the inch. The main floor of the house is 36 by 40 feet, with a rear addition of 20 by 20 feet. The doorways are marked D and the windows W, except two bay windows, which any intelligent carpenter will readily note. We have planned:

K—Kitchen 10x20
C—Closet 4x 8
B—Bedroom 14x20
D—Dining Room..... 14x20
L—Living Room 14x20
P—Parlor 14x20

A porch of 8 feet wide should face the main front of 36 feet.

The figures in the following schedule correspond with the figures on the plan:

1—Double White Flowering Horse Chestnut.
2—Purple leaved Elm (Var. *Stricta Purpurea*.)
3—Purple-leaved Maple.
4—Red Flowering Horse Chestnut.
5—Birch (Var. *Alba Fastigiata*.)
6—Elm (Var. *Campestris Pyramidalis*.)
7—American White Spruce.
8—American Red Spruce.
9—Austrian Pine.
10—White or Weymouth Pine.
11—Norway Spruce.
12—Red Bird or Judas Tree.
13—Enonymus or Strawberry Tree.
14—Purple Fringe.
15—Bladder Senna or *Colutea*.
16—Koelreuteria.
17—Scotch Laburnum.
18—Magnolia Purpurea.
19—Double Flowering Plum.
20—Snow Drop or Silver Bell (*Halesia Tetraptera*.)
21—Hydrangea Paniculata.
22—Scarlet Japan Quince.
23—Syringa Gordoniana.
24—Forsythia Viridissima.
25—Gordon's Flowering Currant.
26—Persian and Chinese Lilacs, each two feet apart.
27—Deutzias of varieties, with Daphne Mezereon, the latter and Deutzia Gracilis being in the front.
28—Upright Honeysuckles, Clethra, Stuartia and Calycanthus are to fill this group. Place the strongest growers in the rear.
29—Spireas, both shrubs and herbaceous.
30—Flowering Lilies, Tulips, Hyacinths, Tube Roses, etc.
31—Weigelas of varieties.
32—Tulip Tree.
33—Pinus Mugho.
34—Juniperus Squamata.
35—Pinus Pumilio.
36—Corsican or Norway Red Pine.
37—Cembrian Pine.
38, 38—Norway Spruces.
39—Cut-leaved Weeping Birch.
40—Scotch Pine.
41—Magnolia Soulangeana.
42—Magnolia Glauca.
43—Rockport Cherry.
44—Elton Cherry.
45—Early Purple Guigne Cherry.
46—Early Richmond Cherry.
47—Black Tartarian Cherry.
48—Red Jacket Cherry.
49—Dwarf Apple, variety Tetofsky on Paradise Stock.

⊕—This indicates the position of Dwarf Pears. Varieties to suit the planter.

※—These indicate positions for grapes. Varieties to please the owner.

Gooseberries and Currants may be planted, if desired, under the shade of the Cherries, being careful not to plant nearer than six feet from the bodies of the trees.

50, 50—The two beds in front of the porch should have the front line planted with Juniperus *Repens*, then immediately back of that, at a distance of one foot from the plants of *Repens*, plant the Juniperus *Nana*. Then fill the balance with one plant each of the following named varieties of Dwarf Evergreens, giving each plant a distance of two feet from its neighbor: *Thuja Ericoides*, Tom Thumb, *Biota Compacta*, *Aurea* and *Pygmea*, *Abies Excelsa Elegans*, *Gregorii*, *Excelsa*, *Mucronata* and *Tortuosa Compacta*, Dwarf Hemlock, (*Canadensis Nana*,) the Yew, (*Taxus Adpressa* and *Ericoides*,) then *Mahonia Aquifolia*, *Berberis Darwinii*, Tree Box, Cotton Taster and Evergreen Thorn, *Cratægus Pyracantha*. At each post of the porch wires should be placed six inches out from them, and one vine each of the following climbers, planted and trained there, viz.: American Ivy, Clematis Virginiana, Wistaria Sinensis and *Lonicera Halleana*.

51—Plant with Geraniums, Heliotropes, Lantanas and other tender flowering plants for the summer. Have ready to take from a place in the rear ground some small plants of Evergreens and place them here for the winter, or obtain leading stems from the tops or branches of old Evergreen trees and stick them in the earth to show a green feature during the winter.

52, 52—These two beds are designed for ever blooming roses. They should be planted 18 inches to two feet apart, according to their habit of growth.

PLAN No. 11.

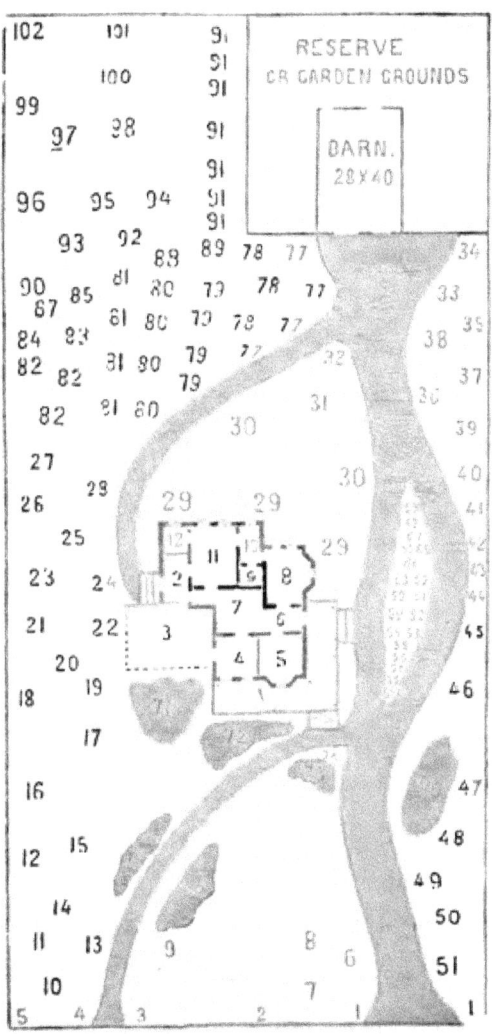

SCALE, 60 FEET TO ONE INCH.

Plan No. 11 is drawn at a scale of sixty feet to one inch, lot 160 by 320 feet, and is designed for a suburban villa lot, or as the front grounds and immediate surroundings of a country farm or fruit grounds with some pretension to style. It is supposed that the house will be of a broken, pointed style, and should stand upon a slight elevation, of say six to eight feet of grade, from the roadway in front. Then if the rear of the house has a high bank or rocky slope, we think our plan will make it of value as well as ornamental, as we have put in trees of good fruit, and yet hardy and ornamental.

The plan of the house, according to our rule, is only the first ground plan, as by it we must know where doors outward, leading to paths, etc., should be constructed. The elevation of the architecture we can do, but as it is not a part or parcel of our plan, we omit it. Reference to the ground plan of the house will show as follows:

1 is a front porch 8 feet wide, passing on the side where the driveway and main entrance to the house is had.

2 is a rear porch with steps, mainly for the use of assistants; it is 8 by 16 feet.

3 is a green-house or conservatory, 20 by 28 feet, with glass doors opening from the hall and a door into room 4, or the Library, which is 15 by 15 feet, and a door into the hall out on the porch, and into the Parlor, room 5, which is 15 by 18 feet; from this room a door opens into the hall, and a bay window, projecting 2 feet and ranging from its main of 12 feet on the level of the wall in the room to eight feet on its front.

6 is the main hall, 8 by 15 feet, where it should have bulwarks each side of one foot, but no door.

7 is a space 16 by 16 feet with a 4 by 4 feet in the rear for entrances from the kitchen and out-of-doors. This space is designed for stairs to the second story. They should be winding, and start at the right as you enter from the hall, so that a view into the green house or conservatory will not be obstructed.

8 is a Dining Room, **16** by **20 feet**, with a bay window. The leading door is from the hall, with connections to 9, the China closet; 10, the Butler's pantry, and 11 the kitchen, 15 by 20 feet, then 12 comes as the kitchen pantry.

WW indicates the windows, and d. the doors. The chimneys are all marked ▄.

13 is the "Porte Cochere" or entrance by carriageway under shelter, 8 by 12 feet.

The following list of trees, etc., against numbers in figure correspond to numbers on the plan, and designate the place in which a tree or shrub should be planted:

1. 1—White-leaved Linden.
2—Purple-leaved Beech.
3—Purple-leaved Elm.
4—Purple-leaved Beech.
5—European Sycamore Maple.
6—Large-leaved Maple.
7—Red Flowering Horse Chestnut.
8—European Mountain Ash.
9—Salisburia or Maiden Hair Tree.
10—Tulip Tree or Liriodendron.
11—Scarlet or Red Maple.
12—English Elm.
13—Mahaleb Cherry.
14—Osage Orange.
15—Deciduous Cypress.
16—Scotch Larch.
17—Cembrian Pine.
18—White or Wymouth Pine.
19—Magnolia Glauca.
20—American White Spruce.
21—Red or Norway Pine.
22—Lawson's Cypress.
23—Corsican Pine.
24—Magnolia Soulangeana.
25—Austrian Pine.
26—Scotch Pine.
27—Norway Spruce.
28—Cucumber Tree.
29, 29, 29—Lombardy Poplars.
30, 30—Norway Spruce.
31—Balsam Fir.
32—American Arbor Vitæ, or American Red Cedar.
33—Black Tartarian Cherry.
34—Red Jacket Cherry.
35—Rockport cherry.
36—Elton Cherry.
37—Early Purple Guigne Cherry.
38—Louis Phillippe Cherry.
39—May Duke Cherry.
40—Early Richmond Cherry.
41—Purple Fringe.
42—Euonymus or Strawberry Tree.
43—White Fringe Tree.
44—Trefoil Tree.
45—High or Bush Cranberry.
46—Hemlock.
47—Weeping Birch (Var. *Elegans Pendula*.)
48—Weeping Cut-leaved Birch.
49—Young's New Weeping Birch.
50—Weeping Mountain Ash.
51—White-leaved Weeping Linden.
52—Siberian Arbor Vitæ.
53—Arbor Vitæ (Var. *Compacta*.)
54—Chinese Golden Arbor Vitæ.
55—Chinese Arbor Vitæ (*Semper Aurea*.)
56—Tom Thumb Arbor Vitæ.
57—Arbor Vitæ (*Globosa*.)
58—Arbor Vitæ (*Ericoides*.)
59—Pinus Mugho.
60—Pinus Mugho Rotundata.
61—Pinus Pumilio.
62—Dwarf Hemlock (*Canadensis Nana*.)
63—Abies To.tuosa Compacta.
64—Abies Excelsa Pygmea.
65—Abies Pumilla Nigra.
66—Savin.
67—Trailing Juniper (*J. Sabina Alpina*.)
68—Juniperus Squamata.
69, 69—Juniperus Repens.

70—Fill this bed as follows: The rear or back line from the road with Weigelas or varieties, set three feet apart and one foot from the edge on the curve. Plant the center with Tree Honeysuckles, Japan Quince and Altheas mixed. Then fill the balance, keeping the front curve in line, with Lilacs, Spireas and Deutzias, with a plant of Hydrangea Paniculata at each end of the bed.

71—This bed is designed for Geraniums, Colens, Lilies, etc., from the green house or conservatory in summer, then filled with Tulips, Hyacinths, etc., for spring blooming.

72—This bed is to have Clematis and Climbing Honeysuckles next to the porch, with everblooming roses in front.

73—Use this bed for Japan Lilies and such other bulbs that bloom, so as to carry the season through.

74—Weeping Juniper (*Oblonga Pendula*.)

75—Plant this bed with Herbaceous Peonias, two or three Tree Peonias in the center, then fill balance with Ivies, Phloxes, etc.

76—Annual flowers or low, bedding out, free-flowering plants.

77, 77, 77, 77—Standard Seckel Pears.

78, 78, 78, 78—Standard Bartlett Pears.

79, 79, 79, 79—Standard Beurre d'Anjou Pears
80, 80, 80, 80—Standard Lawrence Pears.
81, 81, 81, 81—Standard Winter Nelis Pears.
82, 82, 82, 82—Standard Clapp's Favorite Pears.
83—Transcendant Crab Apple.
84—White Winter Crab Apple.
85—Cherry Crab Apple.
86—Coral Crab Apple.
87—Chicago Crab Apple.
88—Hyslop's Crab Apple.
89—Lady Crab Apple.
90—Marengo Crab Apple.
91—Seven varieties of hardy grapes, to be grown on stakes or trained over rocks, as the ground may allow.
92—Dwarf Vicar of Winksfield Pear.
93—Donna Maria Cherry.
94—Chickasaw Plum.
95—Cruger's Scarlet Plum.
96—Wild Goose Plum.
97—Winesap Apple.
98—Gravenstein Apple.
99—Red Canada Apple.
100—Jonathan Apple.
101—Ohio Nonpariel Apple.
102—Maiden's Blush Apple.

The locations of the trees from 83 to 102 must be counted according to the land.

PLAN No. 12.

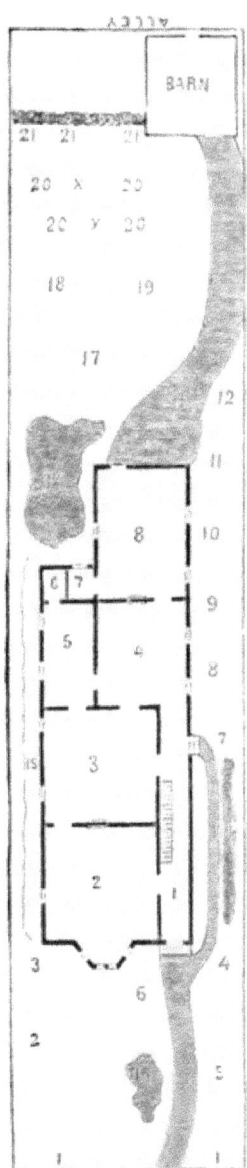

SCALE. 25 FEET TO ONE INCH.

Plan 12 is for a lot 32 by 150 feet, and is drawn to a scale of 25 feet to one inch. This ground plan we have designed for a plain one-and-a-half story house, with the front of the roof to have a triangle in its form, so as to give a little character, which almost any good architect can arrange from a single hint. Referring to it:

No. 1 is a hall 4 by 32 feet; door at front and side.

No. 2 is a parlor, with a wide side window and bay window in front. The room is designed for 16 by 16 feet, the bay window projecting three feet and eight feet on the inside space.

No. 3 is calculated as a family sitting room, 16 by 16 feet, opening into a bedroom, No. 5, of 8 by 16 feet, which is also entered from No. 4, which is to be the breakfast or dining room, which is 12 by 16 feet, and opens from No 8, the kitchen, which is 12 by 16 feet.

From No. 5 there is a closet marked 6, 4 by 4 feet, and from No. 8, marked 7, is a closet 4 by 4 feet.

In making this plan, it is supposed that an alley way runs at the rear, where a barn or stable can be made; or, void of that, an entrance for teams with coal, wood, etc., for the house. landing at the kitchen door.

The following schedule of trees against the figures in numbers indicates the place for each, designated by corresponding numbers on the plan:

1, 1—Cut-leaved Birch.
2—Purple-leaved Beech.
3—Indian Birch (*Betula Bhojpattra*.)
4—Purple-leaved Elm (*Stricta Purpurea*.)
5—Young's Weeping Birch.
6—Cut-leaved Weeping Birch.
7—American White Spruce.
8—Cembrian Pine.
9—American Red Spruce.
10—Corsican, or Red, or Norway Pine.
11—Norway Spruce.
12—Pinus Pumilio.
13—Designed as a form outline to enclose the planting of Spireas, Deutzias, Chinese and Persian Lilacs, Hydrangea Paniculata, and the dwarf varieties of Tree Honeysuckles, with scarlet flowering Quince and Forsythia.
14—Is a bed designed for the planting of what we term half trees, or first-class shrubs, viz.: The Weigelas, Halesia, Euonymus, Dogwood, Purple Fringe, White Fringe, Gordon's Currant, Althea, Berberry, etc. Each plant should stand three feet from the other, and one foot from the edge of the bed. The smallest growing plants should be next the house and the largest at the back.

15—Along this line a border from the house range of one foot, with a slope or grade of two inches from the house; the opposite side should have a grade to meet it, making a rolling water carrier intermediate, and be of turf. The bank next the house should be planted with Geraniums, Petunias, Callas, Heliotropes, Verbenas, etc., for summer blooms, then if the proprietor is able, let the bank next the house be yearly replanted with Hyacinths, Tulips, Crocus, etc.
16—Is a bed to be planted with Perpetual Roses, Geraniums, Verbenas, Heliotropes and annual bulbs, such as Japan Lilies, Tulips, Hyacinths, Gladiolus, etc., may be planted in it.
17—Black Tartarian Cherry.
18—Red Jacket Cherry.
19—Rockport Cherry.
20—Six Dwarf Pears, one each as follows:

Duchesse d'Angouleme. Beurre Giffart.
Louise Bonne de Jersey. Bartlett.
Vicar of Winkfield. Beurre d'Anjou.

21—Three Grapes, varieties as follows:

Telegraph. Concord.
Hartford Prolific.

All the rear of this may be used for whatever suits best the proprietor.

PLAN No. 13.

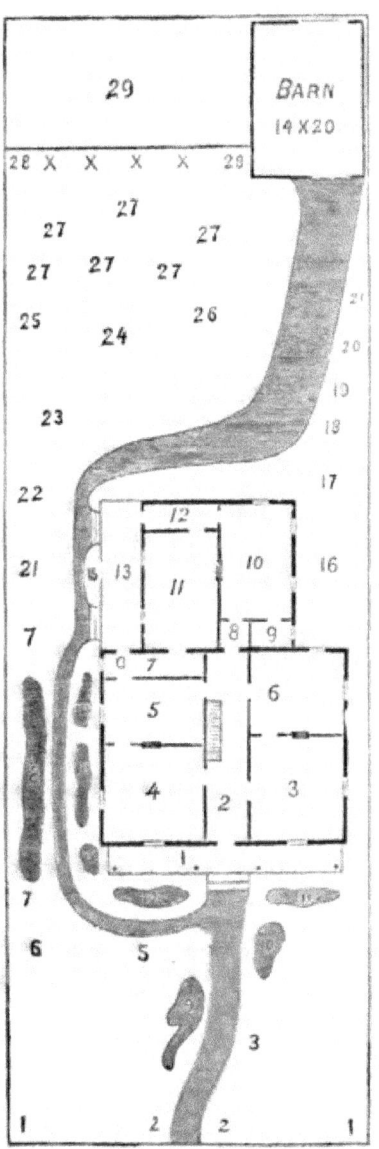

SCALE, 25 FEET TO ONE INCH.

Plan No. 13 is for a lot 50 by 150 feet, with a scale of 25 feet to one inch. The location of the house is 40 feet back from the street. It is supposed to be two stories high with a pointed Gothic roof, three chimneys, a porch in front that should have a railing and flooring, which will make it a resort from the second floor. We give only the ground plan, which we have changed from one made by Rev. D. P. Oakey, Jamaica, Long Island, and originally published in the Horticulturist in 1866, when the writer was a regular contributor. As we have said, we have changed his ground plan, but give his perspective view of elevation.

Perspective of Elevation.

Plan No. 13.

The following is the size and position of the rooms in the ground plan:

No. 1 is the front porch, 6 by 30 feet.

No. 2 is the main hall, 6 by 24 feet, from which the stairs go to the second story; this again opens into a hall, (fig. 7) to back porch (fig. 13), it also enters a hall (fig. 8) 4 by 4 feet, with door to kitchen.

No. 4 is supposed to be a living room, 12 by 14 feet, connecting with a bed room (fig. 5) 8 by 14 feet, and from each of these a door into the main hall, the rear hall and so to the dining room (fig. 11) which is 12 by 16 feet, and entered from the kitccen only through a hall, thus excluding all the bad odors that come from cooking.

The kitchen (fig. 10) is 10 by 16 feet, with a closet 4 by 6 feet.

No. 6 is a room, 10 by 14 feet, connecting with the front room (fig. 3), which we class as the parlor, 14 by 14 feet. No. 6 may be used as a library or private sitting room.

LANDSCAPE GARDENING. 71

In the plan for planting, no carriage-way has been made from the front, but a supposition of knowledge has been entertained that the lot would have an alley in the rear for bringing in coal, etc., and a place for a barn, and we have here placed it 20 by 14 feet, with a driveway for a coal cart, etc., to the kitchen. The scale in which the plan is made must govern all the work, any change from it shall never be acknowledged by the editor of this book, and he who does it shall be prosecuted. I do not hesitate to give credit to whom I am indebted, and the man who steals from me has a record for a future to answer.

Reference to the planting of the grounds is like unto other plans, made by figures of numbers attached to trees, corresponding with the same figures on the plan:

1, 1—Norway Maples.
2, 2—Cut-leaved Beech (*Inclsa*.)
3—Purple-leaved Beech (*Purpurea*.)
4—Magnolia Acuminata or Cucumber Tree.
5—Tulip Tree or *Liriodendron Tulipefera*.
6—Lombardy Poplar.
7, 7—Norway Spruce.
8—This is marked by an outline to be filled with low growing, flowering shrubs, such as Deutzia Gracilis, varieties of Spireas, and Chinese and Persian Lilacs.
9—This bed, marked by outline, should be filled with monthly blooming roses.
10—This bed should have Dwarf Evergreens in it as its center, with Juniperus Repens as its border edging.
11—This bed is designed to be filled in summer with Geraniums, Coleus, etc, and the bulbs, such as Hyacinths, Crocus, etc., planted in autumn for early spring flowering.
12—This bed should correspond with No. 11.
13—Fill this with Hybrid Perpetual Roses.

14, 14—These beds are for annuals or low creeping, ever blooming plants, like the Verbenas, etc.
15—Fill the space with Dwarf Arbor Vitæs and Pines.
16—Black Tartarian Cherry.
17—Rockport Cherry.
18—Red Jacket Cherry.
19—Louise Phillipe Cherry.
20—Early Richmond Cherry.
21—Donna Maria Cherry.
22—Cembrian Pine.
23—American White Spruce.
24—Austrian Pine.
25—Corsican or Red Pine.
26—White or Wymouth Pine.
27—Standard Pears as follows:
 2 Seckels, nearest the road.
 2 Winter Nelis, next back.
 1 Beurre d'Anjou.   1 Bartlett.
 1 Lawrence, without reference to position.
28—Six varieties either of Grapes or Dwarf Apples.
29—Vegetable garden.

PLAN No. 14.

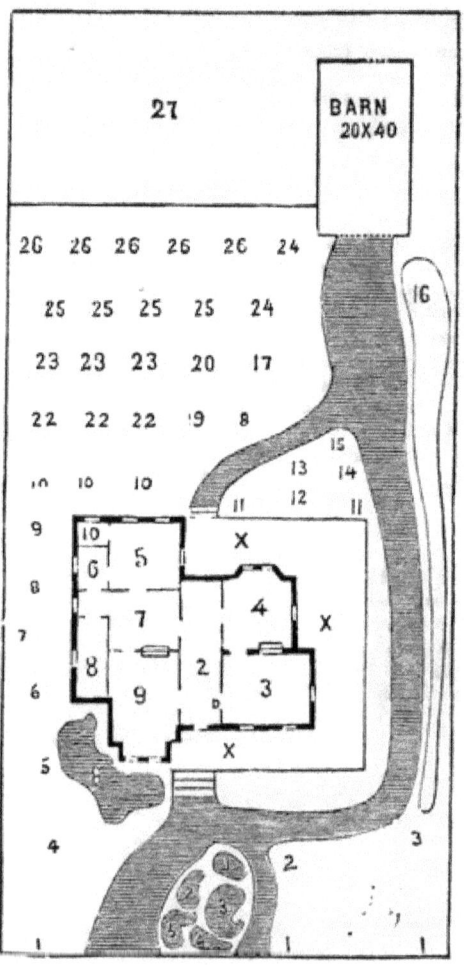

SCALE, 40 FEET TO ONE INCH

References to Plan 14.

First the house is placed forty feet back from the street. The ground plan we have remodeled from one published by H. Hudson Holly, in Harpers' Magazine of May, 1876. The elevation is a copy from Harpers' Magazine of same date, the best magazine ever published.

Now to the ground plan, the scale is forty feet to one inch, and so the porch will vary from 8 to 16 feet; it is marked x x x.

No. 2 is a hall 8 by 28 feet, opening to No. 7, which is designed for the stairway above, and is 12 by 16 feet, with a branch of 4 by 8 feet, having a light of window as a guide to the stairway.

No. 3 is the living room or parlor, 16 by 20 feet, and opening to No. 4, 16 by 16 feet, with a bay window; both of these open by doors to the main hall.

No. 9 is the dining room, 16 by 20 to 22 feet, and opens from the main hall and through No. 7, which is a hall and stairway to No. 5, the kitchen, 16 by 16 feet, with closets (see 6 and 10) then a store room (No. 8) 8 by 20, which can be opened from No. 9. Again, No. 4 can be used as a dining room, and Nos. 9 and 8 as living and bed rooms.

Elevation to Plan No. 14.

Now we show upon the plan the walks and roads by deeper lines and shading. The half oval in front of the house, between the carriage road and foot path, shows bed cut in the turf: these beds, 1, 2, 3, 4, 5, are to be filled with flowering bulbs, plants, etc., according to the taste of the owner. Bed 6 is to be planted with Dwarf Evergreens, the *Juniperus Repens* being the edging.

The trees on this plan are shown as follows:

1, 1, 1—Red or Scarlet Maples.
2—Weeping Cut-leaved Birch.
3—Magnolia Acuminata.
4—Liriodendron Tulipifera.
5—White or Weymouth Pine.
6—Cembrian Pine.
7—American White Spruce.
8—American Black Spruce.
9—Norway Spruce.
10, 10, 10—Lombardy Poplars.
11, 11—Austrian Pine.
12—Scotch Pine.
13—Corsican Pine.
14—Red or Norway Pine.
15—Mountain Pine.
16—This line runs along the roadway and boundary; fill it with hardy flowering shrubs, arranging for the tallest growers to be near the barn, and tone down in their growth to the front.
17—Early Purple Guigne Cherry.
18—Rockport Cherry.
19—Black Tartarian Cherry.
20—Red Jacket Cherry.
22, 22, 22—Standard Bartlett Pears.
23, 23, 22—Standard Beurre d'Anjou Pears.
24, 24—Standard Seckel Pears.
25, 25, 25, 25—Standard Lawrence Pears.
26, 26, 26, 26, 26—Grapes.
27—Vegetable garden.

Designs for School Houses,

and *Plans for the Decoration of the Grounds Surrounding.*

The writer of this work makes no pretensions of being an architect, having studied the subject only in connection with his planting of trees, etc., to make harmony with the surroundings of the house and its order of architecture, but at the suggestion of the enterprising publisher, and with a desire to do what we can for the public good, we have prepared the following. Our country has passed but a hundred years since its day of freedom, yet the education of those who are to come after us becomes the duty of every parent in the land.

The school house, yard and grounds, together with the government of the teacher, in a mild yet decided manner, gives, if made pleasant, a desire to the child to go and learn.

In many of the entirely new sections of the United States, logs can be used, and made even ornamental, for the building. The first settlers of a woody tract have no other resource, but to build log tenements in which to live.

As we write this the *Country Gentleman*, a journal of great value, comes to us, and we venture to take from it an illustration of a log house, with our native wild vines creeping upon it, its dimensions being according to our scale about 16 by 20 feet, which of course can be enlarged.

Such a building as this, placed on dry ground and amid a grove of trees of the native forest, having the old or decayed trees removed, would be daily visited by the children of a neighborhood for learning and with pleasure, all things considered, as before written touching the teacher. We want no more use of the rod, for it is time that intelligence of mind, not passion, should rule. Leaving this we now give an elevation design taken from the *Horticulturist* of 1866, made by G. E. Harney, a capable architect. We have changed his ground plan, and made a plan for the planting of an acre of ground as a school ground, giving the position of the building. We give the lay of the grounds, line of paths, position of the building, but have not space in our columns to give a definite scale for the planting. We number where the large trees are, where the shrubs are to be planted; but first our copy of the building by Mr. Harney as a perspective view.

It will be seen at once, by the most common observer, that the design is to be constructed of boards, set upright, and battened. No show of chimneys has been given by Mr. Harney, and in my change I have marked where the chimneys should be, supposing them only as flues for stove pipe, and opening or ventilating at or in the cupola by side air passages.

The height of the main rooms should be 12 feet, rising in the center of the principal school room, marked 20x30 on the plan, from three to five feet. We quote the following, touching on Harney's ideas relative to the inside structure:

"The wood-work should all be stained, and the walls tinted some soft neutral tint—gray, cream or pearl color. The windows are all sash windows, double hung for purposes of ventilation; and, in addition, there are two ventilating shafts rising from the floor through the attic, and terminating in the ventilator on the ridge of the main roof. These shafts have openings near the floor and ceiling, with arrangements for opening and shutting at will. They are made of smoothly planed, well jointed pine boards, and measure each sixteen inches square inside. In order to keep up the circulation, and to supply cool air from outside, a shaft is introduced, running along under the floor, and terminating at the platform on which, in winter, the stove or heating apparatus will stand, and from this distributed into the room by numerous small holes in the riser of the platform. We consider the simplest methods of ventilation the best, and the above will be found both simple and effective. The great desideratum is to provide means for the discharge of a certain quantity of vitiated air, and to supply its place by the same quantity of pure air, properly warmed in winter. To make the discharge more effective, the stove pipe may be carried up in connection with one of the shafts, rarifying the air, and making the upward current stronger, but in ordinary cases this will be hardly necessary.

There are two entrances to this house, one for boys and one for girls. Both entries are ten feet apart, and are in the main building, opening directly into the school room.

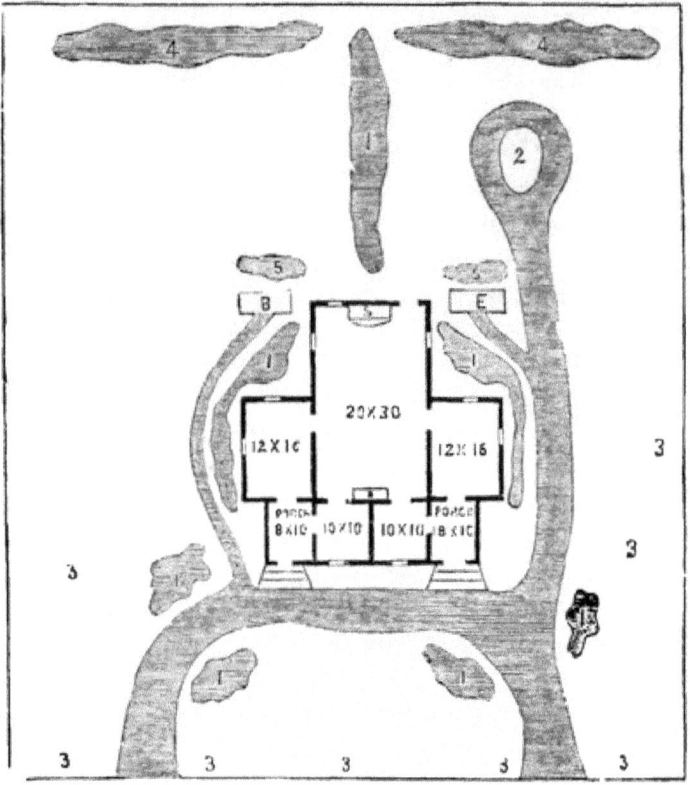

And now to our change of the ground plan. We make A as the teacher's stand; s, the position for the main stove; ss, in each of the 12x16 rooms, both of which to be used as class rooms; c c, the position of the flues for the stove pipes. We have laid out our paths on the ground to be ten feet wide from the front gate, sixteen feet directly in front of the center of the house. The rear line carriage path, for the delivery of fuel, and accommodation of those who take their children to school on a rainy day, we grade, as the lines show, from ten to eight feet. The porches are indicated on the plan, and the rooms 10x10 are for the clothing of the children, one for the girls and one for the boys. In the rear we have marked B and C as for two privys, and have made our plan that the boys should enter and use mainly the side where the twin roadway is shown. The outlines of beds on the plan, marked 1, are for hardy flowering shrubs, both evergreen and deciduous. 2 is a Norway Spruce; the remainder of the half oval to be in turf. 3 are for deciduous forest trees, provided the front of the lot faces the east or south. If the lot faces the north or north-west, these should be changed to large evergreens, like White Pine, Norway Spruce, Scotch Pine, etc.

The outlines of beds marked 4 should have mingled evergreens planted eight or ten feet apart, if that line be to the north. On the contrary, if to the south, it should be planted with second class growth of deciduous trees, mingled with dwarf evergreens in the fore ground. 5, 5, should be of Norway Spruce, Arbor Vitæ, etc., as a screen from the outhouses. All the land beside what and where we have named should be in turf.

Hedges and Screens.

Nothing, perhaps, to the lover of Nature, adds so much to the cheerful aspect of a district as the hedges by which it is intersected, and the timber and other trees with which it is clothed. The latter stand out in bold relief in the picture, while the hedges fill up those necessary lines, without which there would be a certain amount of blank. A good hedge is, in many instances, a farmer's pride, and in this respect he looks at it in a different light from the admirer of rural scenery, to whom the more crooked the hedge, and the more heterogeneous the plants of which it is composed, the more beautiful it appears; while to the farmer, a hedge occupying the least possible space of ground, straight in its outline, and forming an impassable boundary to cattle, is the approach to perfection which he delights in. The hedge is always a prominent feature, not only of beauty, but of usefulness on the borders and grounds of the owners of suburban villas.

Screens also are features of value upon all places, and of them hereafter.

During the last thirty years great progress has been made in this direction, and we may expect to see still farther advances. In many districts, however, owing to gross error in the use of plants, or in the case of cutting and pruning hedges once planted have, as it were, disappeared; yet, hedges have their uses, and I hope yet to see their general adoption over the large breadth of our goodly land, much of which is now sub-divided by wire, board or rail fences, a constantly yearly drain upon the owners. No hedge, planted with a view to form a barrier, should be planted with varied trees, nor with trees or plants liable to sucker or throw out lateral roots long distances, thereby making the keeping clean the land fully up to the line of the hedge. The Maple, Elder, Willow, and various other trees have been used, but always unsatisfactorily. The Osage Orange has failings that have rendered it of little value in many sections. The Thorn and

Wild Plum have both been tried, but without favor. The Honey Locust is a tree of perfect hardihood, has no suckers, or long, lateral roots, bears the shears perfectly, and its thorns aid in its forming a perfect barrier. We look upon the Honey Locust as the best plant for forming a farm or road side hedge that is grown in this country. Hedges, apart from their utility, are a necessary feature of the landscape in most districts. The want of them where high cultivation exists, causes a sad blank in the winter scenery; but it is not in these cases only that we advocate their adoption, for their value on many of the large tracts of land on the prairies and other sections, would be of interest and value to all. All of this change of varieties of plants to be used for hedges we look upon as coming to us, and in such manner that no hesitation to plant, or care to cultivate, will remain.

FORMING OF HEDGES.

All of the subject matter of instruction as to how to plant hedges, may be told in a few words, and will apply as well to one variety of plant as to another. The whole is, *first*, to have good soil free from any standing water. *Second*, make a trench where the hedge is to stand, two feet wide and eighteen inches deep, throwing out all the earth; then dig the earth at the bottom of said trench eight to twelve inches deep; then throw the best of soil over the bottom to a depth of two inches. *Third*, select the plants so that in planting they will all be of one size; then plant (carefully, by spreading the roots and working earth of the best kind among them), at distances varying according to the plants, of 16 to 18, or 20 to 24 inches from plant to plant, covering the upper roots about four inches deep in the trench, and finish by leaving the ground nearly level with its adjacent.

PLANTING FOR SCREENS.

The planting of trees to act as a screen to a building, or protection of a garden or orchard, varies from that of hedges only in placing the trees at greater distances apart.

VARIETIES OF TREES.

The Honey Locust, or *Three Thorned Acacia*, **Osage Orange**, and **Buckthorn**, are the only three deciduous plants that we recommend for permanent hedges as barriers. The first and last named may be relied upon in almost any section of our country; but the Osage Orange is, in many locations, unsuited, because from extreme cold it is liable to kill out. Fancy hedges of various flowering shrubs are frequently made as boundaries to garden or road line, where cattle are not pastured. These like the varieties of evergreens, cannot be depended upon as barriers of protection. Among evergreens, the Norway Spruce and the varieties of Arbor Vitæ are most commonly used and popular; but all evergreens will bear the shears in the pruning, so that the planter may choose variety at his pleasure. The practice of alternating varieties in the row is often equally as good as one distinct variety, while it gives a unique, characteristic appearance to the line. For instance, the Norway Spruce and American Black Spruce are planted alternately; so also Hemlock alternate Cembrian Pine or Lawson's Cypress, where the latter will bear the winter. The American White Spruce, White Pine, Corsican Pine, each and all are good.

Where trees are planted for screens, to grow twelve to twenty feet high, they should be at least two and a half feet apart; and it is often better to make the line a little irregular, by placing an additional tree of another variety some three or four feet back of the main line. Dwarf hedges of evergreens are sometimes planted, or may be to mark the boundary of a flower garden or croquet ground, etc. Varieties of the Box, Evergreen Thorn, Junipers, Kalmias and Yews may be used with certainty in many sections, but the Mahonia is not always an evergreen, but a sub-evergreen.

Winter Decoration
of Open Grounds and in the House.

As winter approaches come thoughts as to the manner by which the front grounds, where now are beds of blooming flowers, can be made features of attractive and agreeable beauty during the coming winter. Again comes the question of "How to cheaply have some green-foliaged plant in the window all the winter?" In the house of the wealthy, where a steady heat is kept up night and day, almost any plant can be grown; but my notes are for those who perhaps keep no steady fire night and day, in any one room, and the removal daily of plants subject to

No. 1.

damage from frost, is a task that is labor, and often forgotten so; that when morn comes the Geranium, or other tender flowering plant, has little or nothing left to pleasantly greet the eye. To remedy this, in the house, let me say, make a box the length of width of the window in which you wish it to stand, one foot wide, ten inches deep. Make the bottom board of the box with grooves, to carry the water to one point for outlet; next put inside a false bottom board, having quarter inch holes in it, once every four inches—this false bottom board to be two inches above the lower one. Place flat stones, broken to two inches, or thereabouts, upon the bottom; the two inches of good garden soil, and for working in among roots to be planted herein, get good leaf mould, i. e., the soil next under the turf of an old grass pasture, or the soil from ground where an old wood-pile has been. Now plant, next to the outside border of this box, with varieties of Sedums and Lysimachia, alternately; next, inside plant of Juniperus Repens and Nana, using Nana as corner plants; next, one plant each of Pinus mugho rotundata, at each end of the box, inside of the Junipers; next plant two of Taxus adpressa and two of Taxus cricoides; next, one at each end, inside of the last, of Evergreen Thorn, and finish with center plant of Hemlock, Lawson's Cypress, or some dwarf Arbor Vitæ. These, when planted with the earth up to within half an inch of the surface—that covered with fine moss will, with care in watering, keep green and fresh all winter, and in the spring the plants can be used in the open ground. We have often visited rooms where ferns and many delicate climbing vines were growing in glass cases, without any extra heat other than what might come from an open grate or wood fire place. Flora's admirers are more than even the most ambitious flirt—if there is such a creature—could desire; but her gems, i. e., Flora's, are not all made of flowers. Foliage is a gem, without which many of her most brilliant colors would not be noticed. Contrast, it is said, makes harmony, but such is not always the case; yet the shades of green that belong to foliage always give a pleasing contrast with the flower, no matter what its color.

We have seen in the center of a window a fancy piece of rock work, formed upon a common plank, grooved, so that all water should run to one outlet. Broken rocks of selected colors, or what some term rough, ungainly moss, overgrown boulders, laid up in resemblance of some rocky point or mound one has seen in their wanderings, and mingled with them, leaf mould, or good loamy, sandy soil (not peat from a low, swampy bog); into which plant varieties of ferns and hardy creeping vines, such as the Chinese Evergreen Honeysuckle, Ampelopsis Veitchii, German Ivy, Vincas of varieties, Pilea reptans, rose and lemon scented Geraniums, some of the hardy Salvias, Mahonias, Creeping Junipers, Daphne Mezerium. The whole forms a most pleasing feature in a room, and is of far less trouble than plants grown in pots, to be changed, repotted, etc., from time to time. Another feature of this style of house decoration of Flora's gems, is, that the roots are rarely injured by moisture or draught, even if too often or too rarely watered.

No. 2.

From this we revert to the common practice of window decoration with pot plants and hanging baskets filled with creepers, whose graceful lines oft wave so thick and fresh in the life as to give an idea that they are like the Mistletoe, living only upon air, while they call lovers to them, under the impression that what may there be said shall come to pass.

Through the kind courtesy of James Vick, Esq., we copy from his *Floral Guide* some illustrations of how to arrange plants and hanging baskets in the window.

No. 1 represents two windows on each side of a mirror, with plants in pots, and hanging baskets. This is apparently given for outside than inside show.

No. 2 shows the plants in pots, and mostly upon the floor; less of hanging plants than of erect form.

No. 3.

No. 3 is a tasteful arrangement of plants and vines, in a bay window; yet we think a cased box for the roots of plants under the window-sill, and the climbers planted to run upon fine wires over the casings, with here and there a shrubby plant in the center, or along the window lights, would be more natural. The vase is excellent, and so the hanging baskets; but as we have before said, there is generally too much care and attention required in this matter to meet the resources of a majority with whom purity and truth are always in association with earth's productions of beauty, and thus a forethought of a future paradise.

No. 4 is a presentation which rarely can be found, inasmuch as the form of the window, with the heavy stile in center, is not generally found in residences of those who cannot depend upon a green house to supply plants.

No. 4.

Mr. Vick gives some good and sensible remarks in his *Floral Guide*, touching Bulbs, and we refer those who desire to grow bulbs, to his work; nor do we believe in delicate plants next a window, where the temperature causes frost to congeal in icy flakes upon the outside of the glass, no matter what may be the inside heat. In the care of plants in windows or sitting rooms, care should be always taken to keep the earth moist, yet not wet. Water with rain water; never use limestone water from a well. The time to water is generally best just about sunset. Where plants are grown in pots or boxes, the covering the surface with patches of moss taken from decaying wood in the woods, or from moss covered rocks, tends to keep an even temperature in the soil. Another good principle and practice is to insert the crock in which the plant grows, into another, so much larger that it will leave one quarter inch of space around it, and one inch at bottom; fill this space with finely pulverized charcoal, placing more or less of fine pebbles in the bottom to secure the drainage from the main pot. Some mingle clean sand with the charcoal; this tends to keep the earth around the roots of the plants from immediate direct changes from moisture to drought; or when watering the plants a light watering of the line of charcoal should be given. Avoid the use of guano or other stimulating manures; but let the rain water with which you water always be of a tepid warmth, but if it can be so, from the sun's rays. Where plants are left open in the room, they should be covered with a light cloth or paper, during the process of sweeping or dusting. Flora loves cleanliness.

It is unadvisable to grow a great variety of plants in the house. Many that are beautiful under the regular temperature and care of the greenhouse, prove of no value when placed in the changeable atmosphere and dust of a living room.

OUSTIDE WINTER GARDENING.

Lawns or front door yards, as often called, where beds of flowers have been during the summer, may be kept in good appearance at a cheap rate, by obtaining from the woods or from waste trees in nurseries, branches of evergreens of varieties, and setting the ends in the ground, arranging the heights as well as shades of foliage to give a pleasing effect. Another way is to obtain small plants, varieties of evergreens, and plant them, mulching the ground around and between them. These can be removed in spring, set in a shady place, and used again the coming winter.

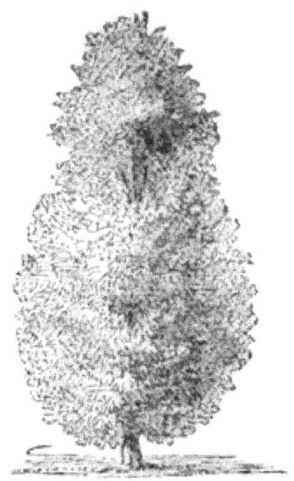

Magnolia Acuminata.

Magnolia Glanca.

For descriptions see pages 31 and 32.

NORWAY SPRUCE.

For description see page 22.

AUSTRIAN PINE.

For description see page **21**.

HEMLOCK SPRUCE.

For description see page 22.

EUROPEAN SILVER FIR.

For description see page 21.

LAWSON CYPRESS.— *Cupressus Lawsoniana.*

For description see page 20.

INDEX.

	PAGE.

A
Annuals... 5
Amateur Landscape Gardening................................ 1

B
Bedding Plants.. 15

C
Cuttings of Shrubs and Plants............................... 13

D
Deciduous Trees and Shrubs.................................. 8
Description of Trees, Shrubs, &c......................... 19 to 24

E
Evergreens... 14 to 17

F
Fine Arts in Landscape Gardening............................ 5
Flower Gardening.. 4
Fountain... 60
Fruits—desirable varieties................................. 50

G
Garden Soil... 8
Grass Lawns.. 10
Ground—keep the surface loose.............................. 10
    view of.. 56
Gardening, Winter.. 88

H
Hollyhocks... 14
Herbaceous Plants.. 15
Hardy Annuals.. 15
Hedges and Screens... 80

L
Lilies... 15 and 16
Landscape Adornment................................... 56 to 59
Lawns... 9
    Grass.. 10
    the making of....................................... 9

M
Mulching Trees... 43

P
Plan No. 1.—Lot 30×150 feet................................ 43
Plan No. 2.—How to improve a place......................... 45
Plan No. 3.—Lot 100×300 feet............................... 47
Plan No. 4.—Lot 50×150 feet................................ 49

INDEX.

Plan No. 5.—Corner lot, 100×200 feet. 52
Plan No. 6. — For a large lot from 5 to 500 acres 53
Plan No. 9.—Lot 100×200 feet. 61
Plan No. 11.—Lot 160×320 feet. 63
Plan No. 12 — Lot 32×150 feet. 67
Plan No. 13.—Lot 50×150 feet. 69
Plan No. 13.—Perspective of elevation. 70
Plan No. 14 —Ground plan 72
Plan No. 14.—Elevation. ....73 and 74
Perennials. 14
Pruning Trees in Spring. 11
Pruning Trees in Winter 12

R

Rural Home Adornments. 5
Rolling Walks and Roads. 8
Roses, propagation 13
Removing Trees, &c. 17

S

Seed for Lawns 9
Shrubs, under drip of trees 12
    Hardy 13
    Condensed Description of. ....17 to 42
    Ornamental Deciduous. 38
    Condensed Description of Ornamental. 39
School Houses. ....75 to 79
Screens, Planting. 81
Suburban Residence for a gentleman. 47

T

Turfing New Grounds. 8
Trees, protect the crowns. 11
    Pruning in Spring. 11
    Winter pruning 12
    Plow up to the roots. 12
    Bush and pyramid. 12
    Condensed Descriptions of. ....17 to 42
    Weeping Deciduous. 22
    Deciduous. ....25 to 38
    Varieties for Hedges and Screens. 82
    Transplanting, Evergreens, &c. ....17 and 18
    Illustrations of choice varieties. ....89 to 94

W

Walks and Roads. 7
Walks and Ground Plan. 58
Winter Decoration. ....83 to 88

www.ingramcontent.com/pod-product-compliance
Lightning Source LLC
Chambersburg PA
CBHW032239080426
42735CB00008B/918